Reviews for *That Book* series and David Conley

A totally delightful, energetic and imaginative book. For lovers of the ancient world, young and old!

Ursula Dubosarsky, Author of over 50 books and Australian Children's Laureate 2020-2021

Whenever Terry and I take our time-travelling rubbish bin for a spin through the ancient mythical lands of Greece or Midgard, we always take David Conley as our guide- and if he's not available then we take one of his books. He's the most knowledgeable expert on Greek and Norse mythological figures we've ever met, and we've met them all!

Andy Griffiths, author of over 30 books including the critically acclaimed Treehouse series

My character was pointless.

Circle

Some of the best books I have read and very funny.

Aaron, 8

David Conley is a bigger legend than Odin and a bigger marvel than Marvel! He puts the Rock into Ragnarök and the Norse into Norsænivegavinnuverkfæraskúrinngullhringur!!!! This is how the Greeks would have illustrated their myths and legends and it's what the Norse gods really looked like! Trust me, I've asked them.

I loved reading his mythologies - though I had to build a wooden horse and hide inside it to sneak into my son's room to get the books off him to read them.

Dr Craig Cormick OAM, award-winning author of over 40 books for the young and young at heart.

My character was very 2-dimensional,

Triangle

I like all the short stories... I really like it... I never want to stop reading it... I just want to read it forever... it's really good.

Harry, 5

Definitely my favourite book that I've read then read again... Mum when is the next book out?

Will, 7

My whole part was removed from the final cut of this book!

Shape of a Duck in Swim Shorts

Your books are the best! I read them over and over, Mum says they are value for money. Your drawings have so much detail and the characters seem so alive (even though some are actually dead). I love learning about mythology and I can even pronounce all the titans and gods names better than my Dad (and spell them correctly too).

Josh, 8

That David Conley is a fantastic writer. All families should have his books. They're perfect for anyone aged 5 to 2 761 years, or when they die, whichever comes first.
Giselle, 12

As a teacher librarian, I am always looking for ways to engage students in reading and even reading about non-fiction topics. Ever since I have had David's books in the library, well they are never really in the library because they are always loaned out. What can I say? Children are really drawn to the imaginative ways these books are presented.

Marion, Teacher Librarian

I feel like my character got a bit of a rough treatment,

Texture

There's no better feedback for this book then seeing a contented 7 year old boy curled up on the couch engrossed in the hilarious illustrations and intriguing tales. In his words the book is 'very unusual and very interesting'. In my words it's a unique, colourful and irreverent spin on some very old stories. He turns dusty into dazzling. I don't know many Greek myths, and I blame my misfortune on being born before David was sharing his talent with the world!

Emma, Playwright

That Book About Drawing Stuff

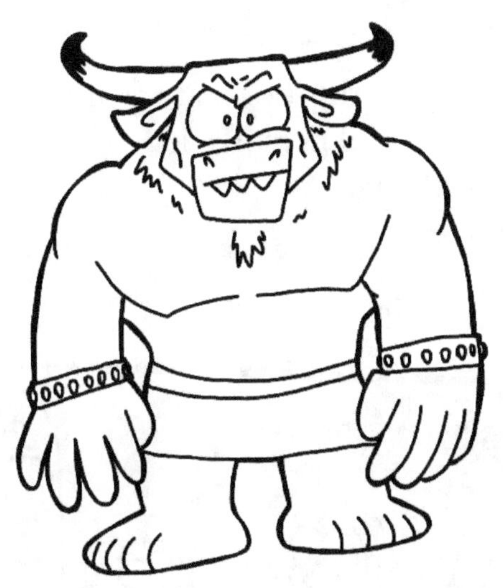

David Conley

Dedicated to my three favourite people...

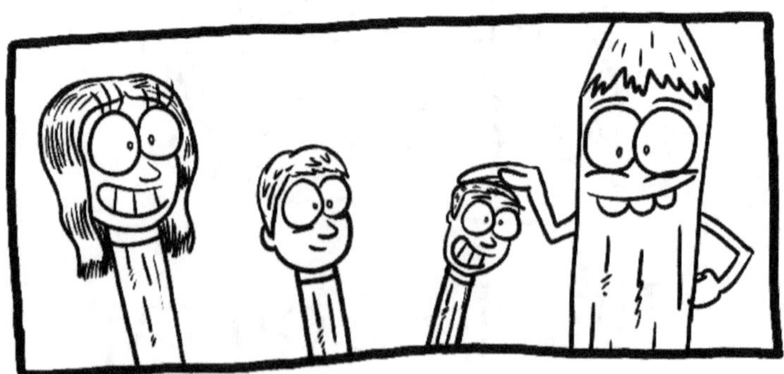

Contents

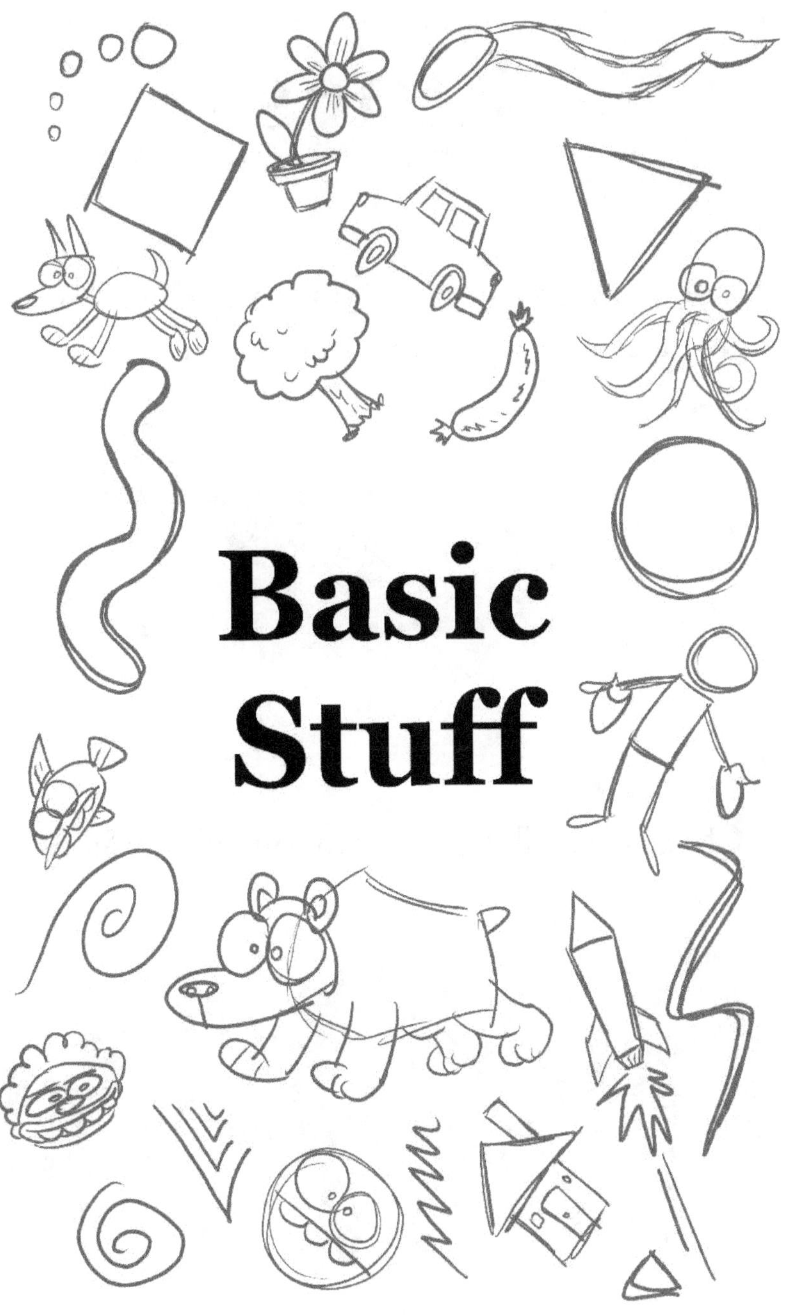

Basic Stuff

Lines

You're mostly going to draw using light lines by pressing very lightly on the page.

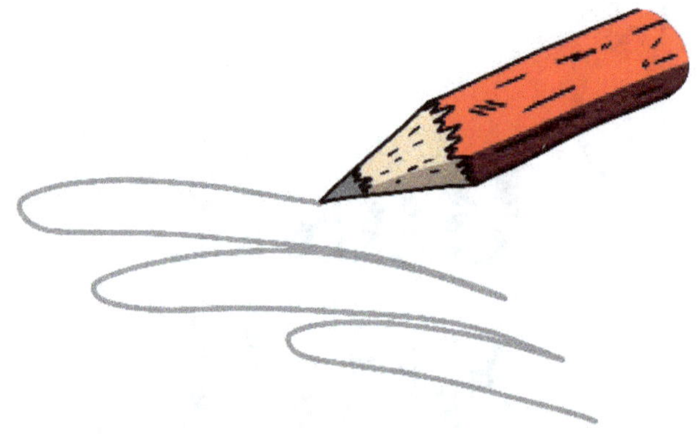

Challenge: fill a page with lots of light lines.

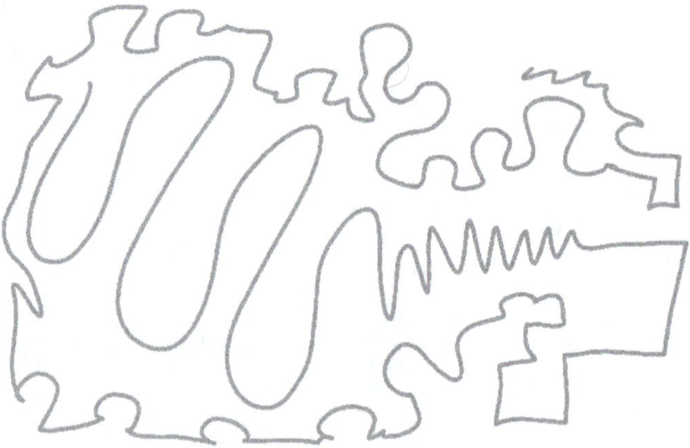

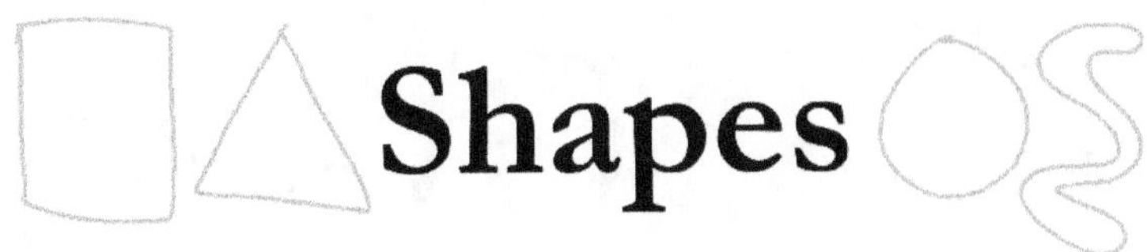

Shapes

I like to use **squares**, **circles**, **triangles** and **sausages** in my pictures (none of them are perfect, of course)

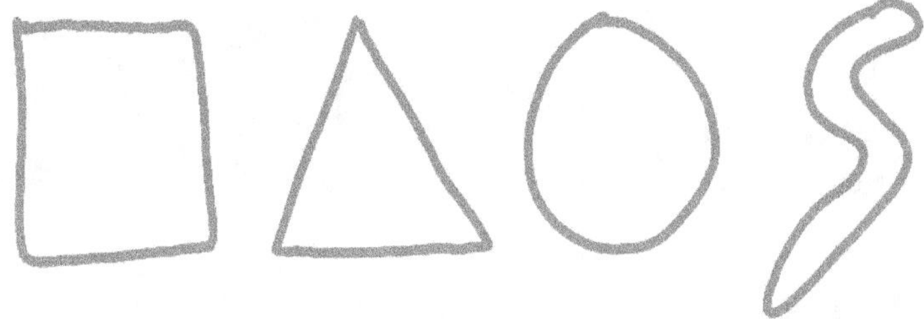

The squares can be any shape with 4 sides and 4 corners…

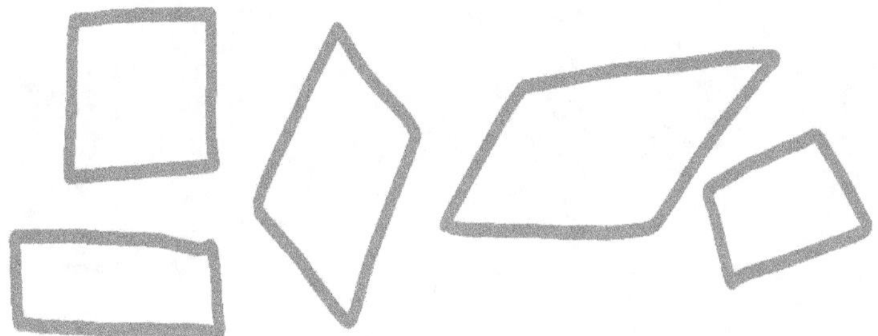

The circles can be any round shape…

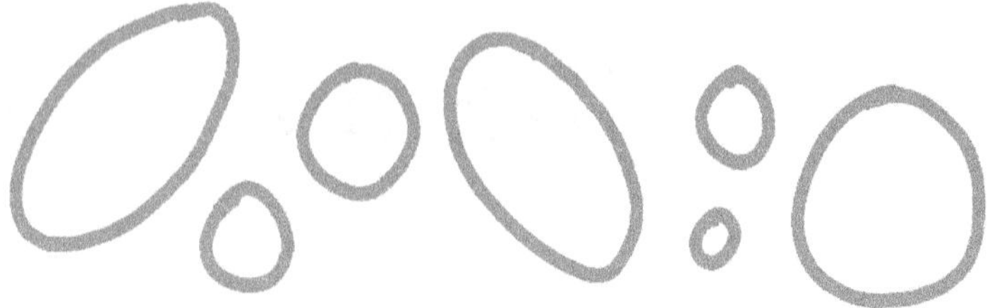

And when I say sausages, I mean any bendy shape with round ends.

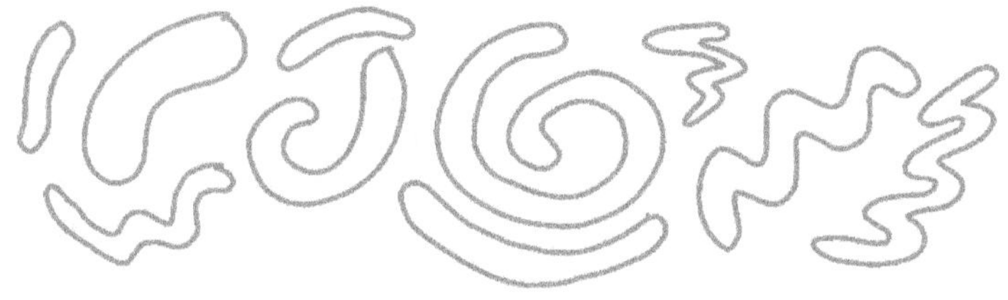

Challenge: Draw lots and lots of different squares, triangles, circles and sausages and draw them all with light lines!

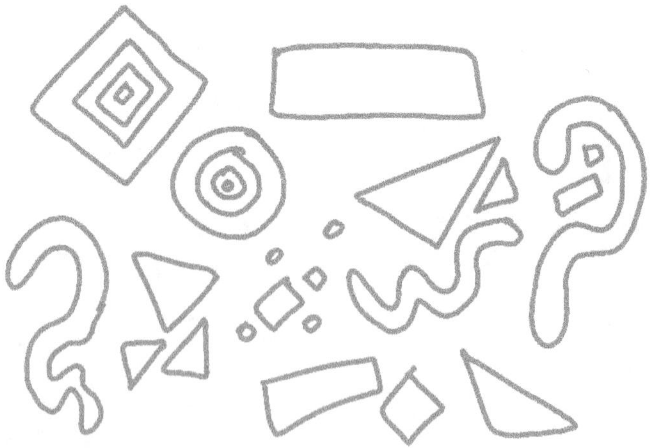

Structures

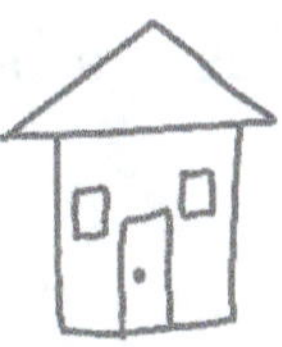

You can stick shapes together to make lots of different structures. Like this…

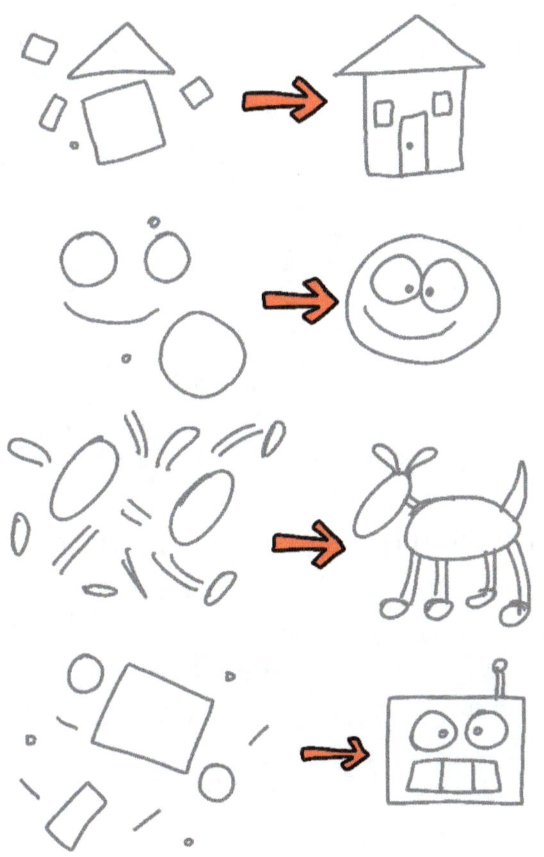

When you make structures, be brave with the shapes you use!

This is a house with a square as its base.

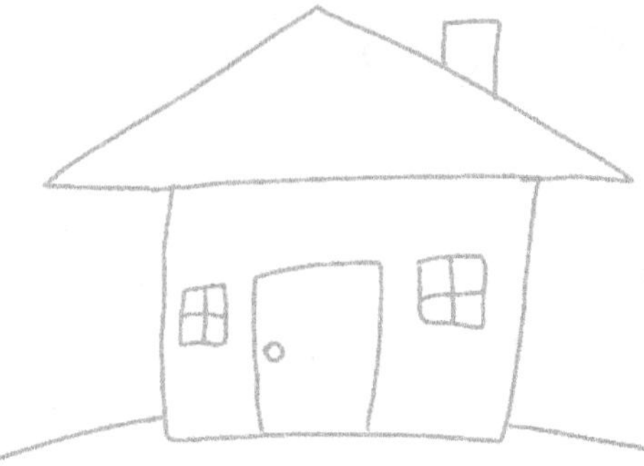

And this is a house with a circle as a base.

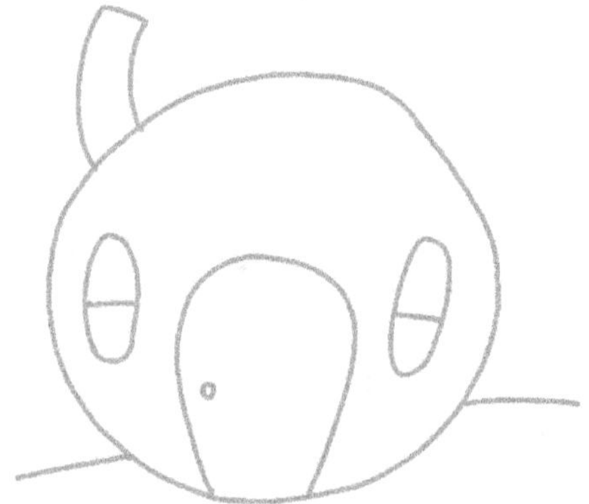

This house has a sausage as its base.

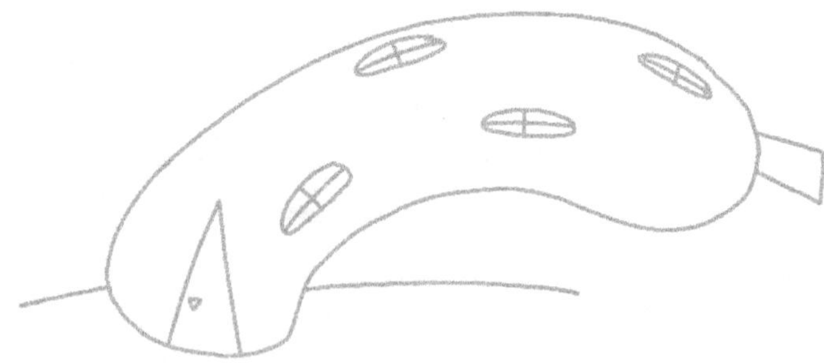

Challenge: Have a go at using shapes to build as many things on this list as possible.

dog	house	car
tree	elephant	frog
robot	rocket	gecko
monkey	igloo	jet
hippo	bike	lion
truck	kite	net
octopus	pineapple	queen
rhino	slime	T.V.
umbrella	vulture	walrus
yak	zebra	aeroplane
beehive	cat	dragon
eagle	flames	gorilla
helicopter	ice cream	jail cell
cage	kangaroo	lemon
bug	spider	phone

Remember to use light lines!

Details

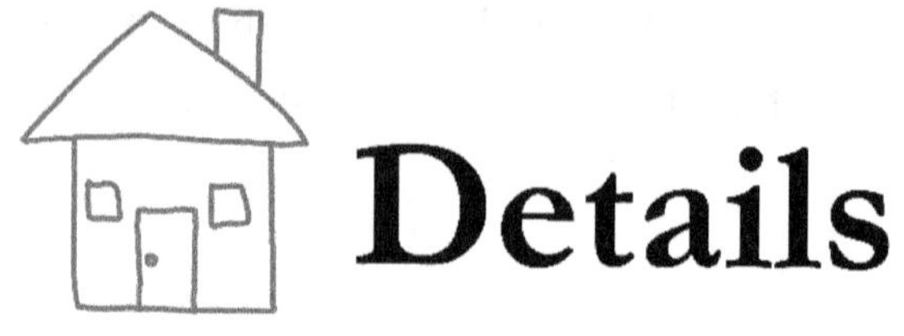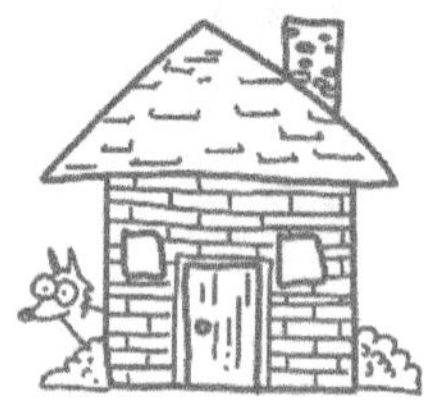

Details are the smaller bits you add to stuff to make it look more interesting or special.

Here's what details can do to a house structure...

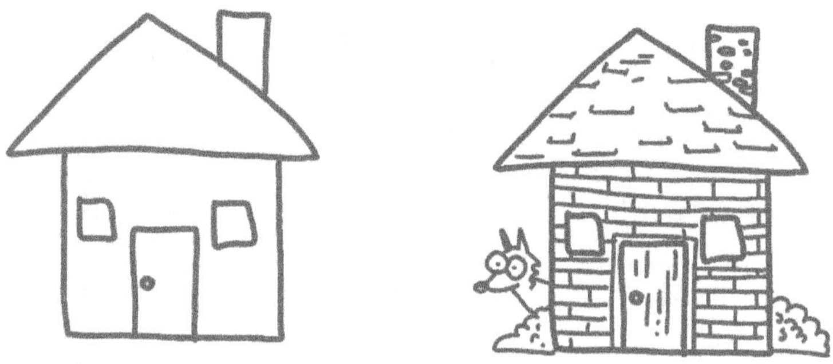

Here's what details can do to a person structure...

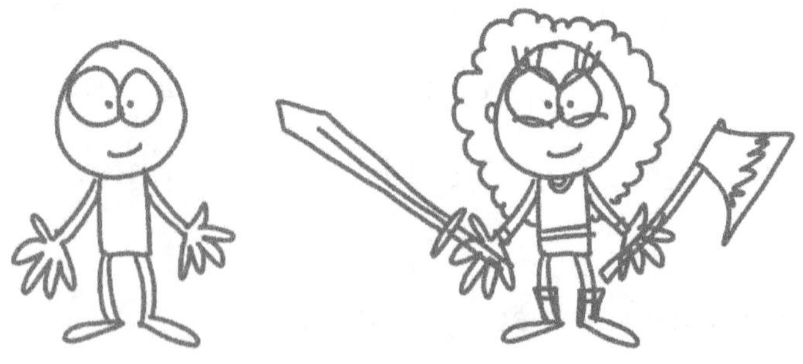

When I add details, I usually add them by size…

The biggest detail is added first.

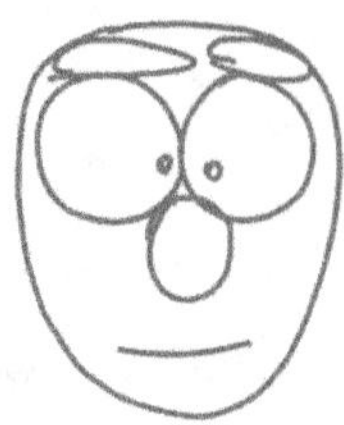

Then the next biggest.

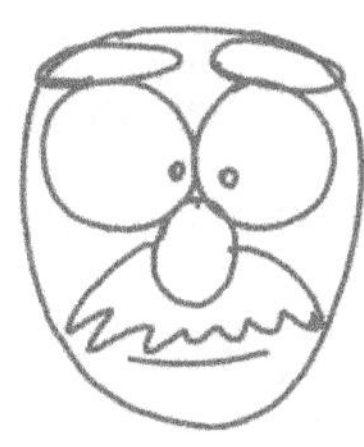

And so on…

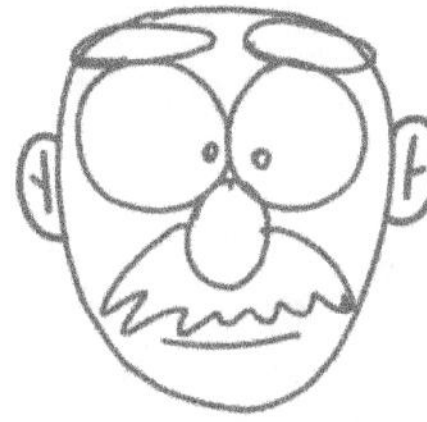

And so on…

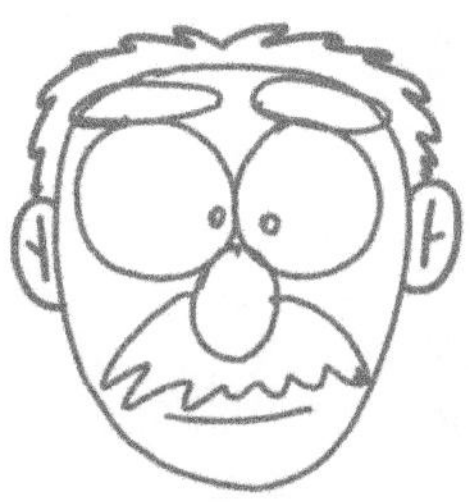

(You get the idea)

Challenge:

Draw the same structure 3 times then add details to make each structure look different.

Texture 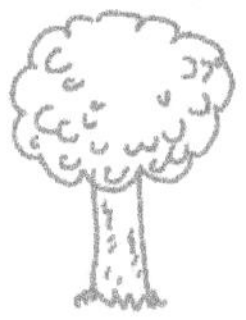

Textures are the little lines and swirls that tell you how something would feel if you touched it.

Here are some different lines and swirls that give different feels.

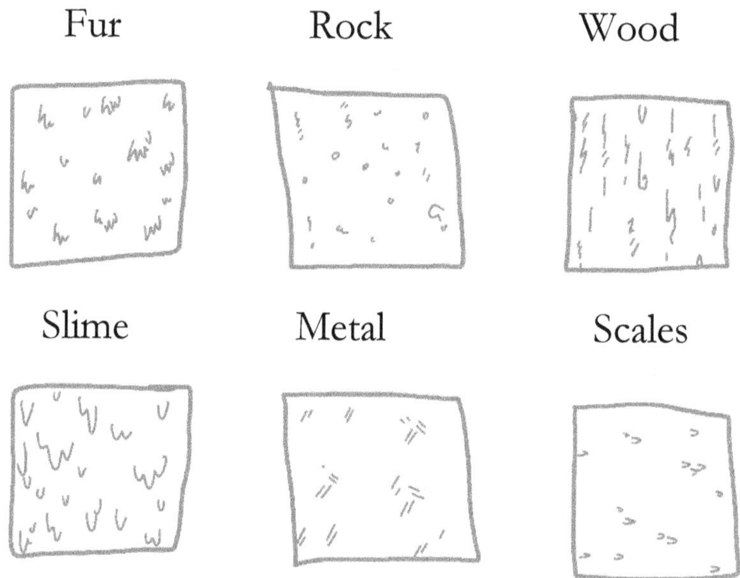

Challenge:

Try drawing something with details and different types of textures.

Inking

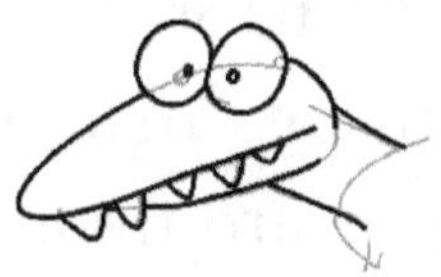

Inking is when you start with a light lined picture like this:

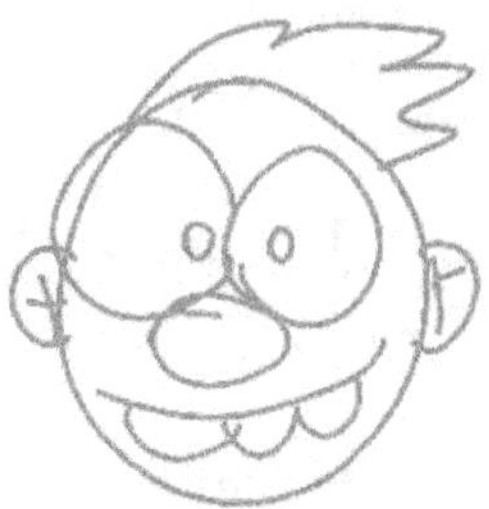

Then trace over the lines with a texta or pen to make them stand out. Like this:

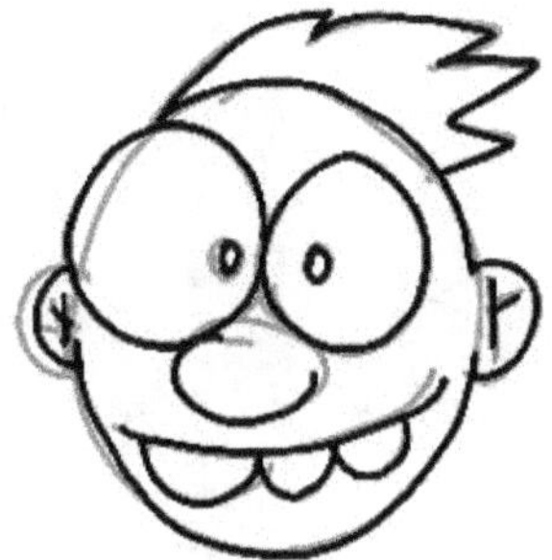

Then use an eraser to get rid of the pencil lines and make your picture look like this:

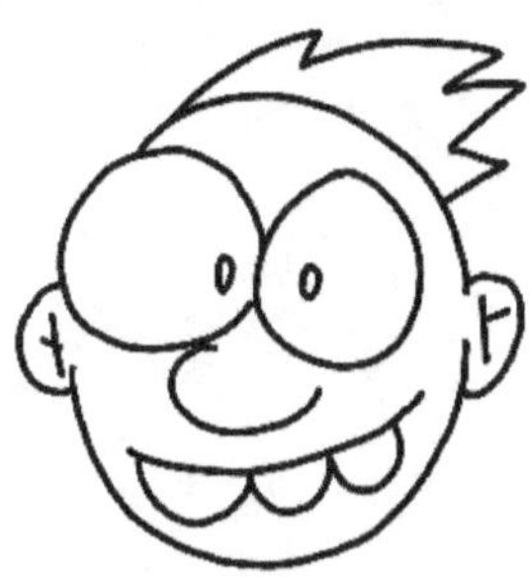

What happens if you want to ink something with bits that are far away and close like on this lizard thing I just drew?

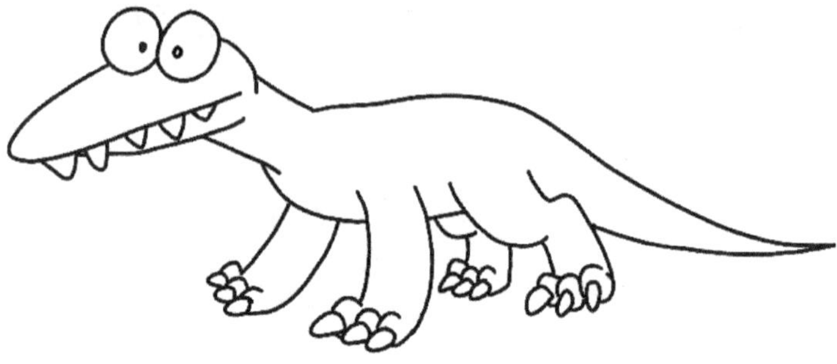

You just go front-to-back.

Here it is step-by-step on the lizard thing.

First we draw the lizard with light lines using a pencil:

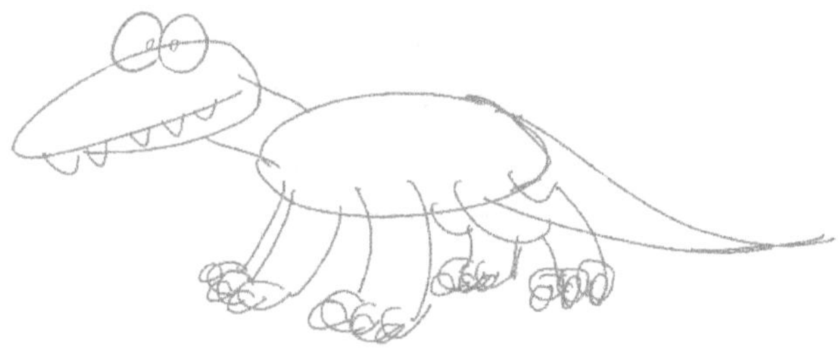

Then we ink the closest thing on the lizard (which are the eyes):

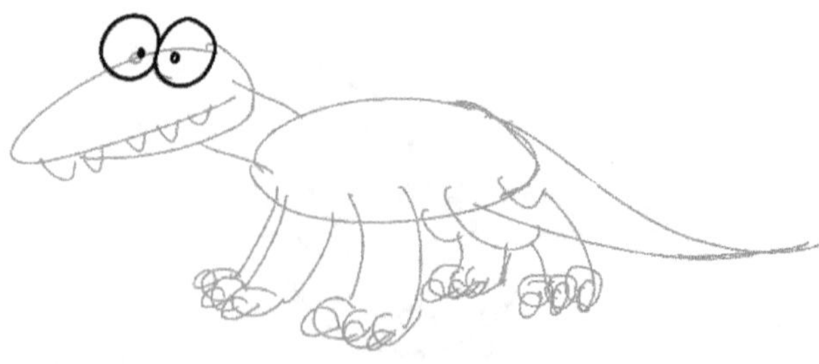

Then ink the next thing back (which is the top part of the head):

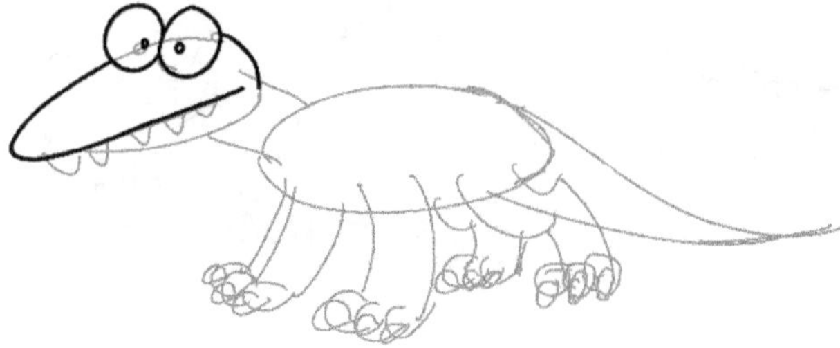

Then you keep inking stuff moving slowly from the front to the back of the lizard:

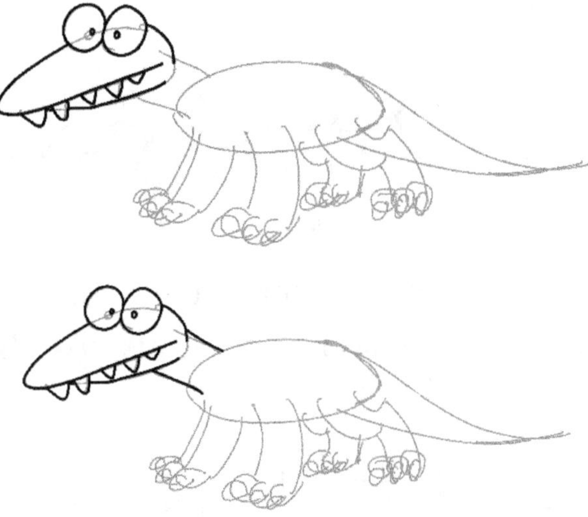

These two legs are in front of the rest of the body so you ink them both next:

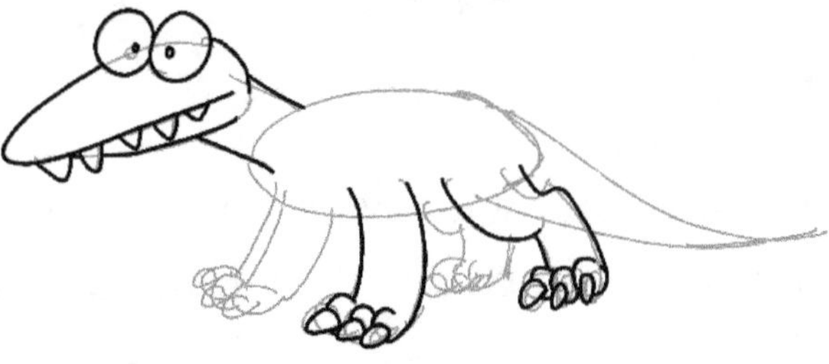

The rest of the body and the tail are next:

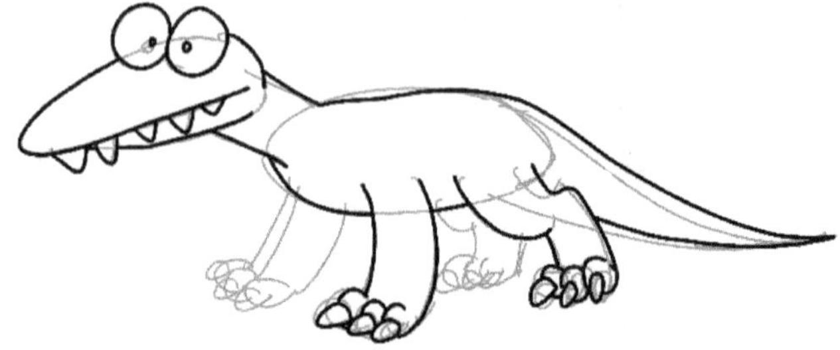

Those last two legs at the back are the tricky ones, you'll ink them last:

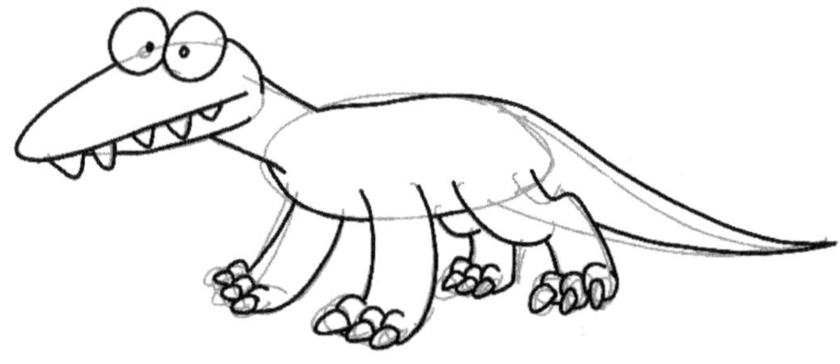

Then you erase your pencil lines and your picture will have some layers, just like this:

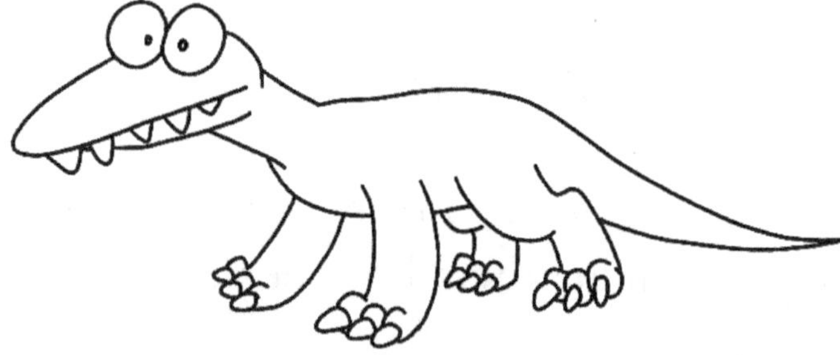

Challenge:

Draw something with details and texture (maybe even some layers) then ink it.

Inking Crowds

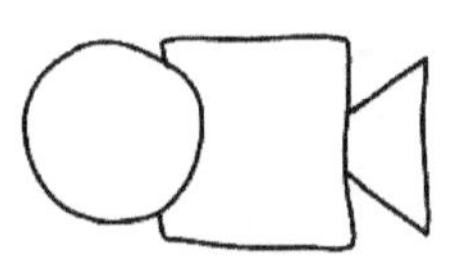

Your next step is to draw and ink a picture with a crowd (I just call any picture with lots of stuff in it a crowd).

Here's a crowd of three shapes- a circle, a square and a triangle...

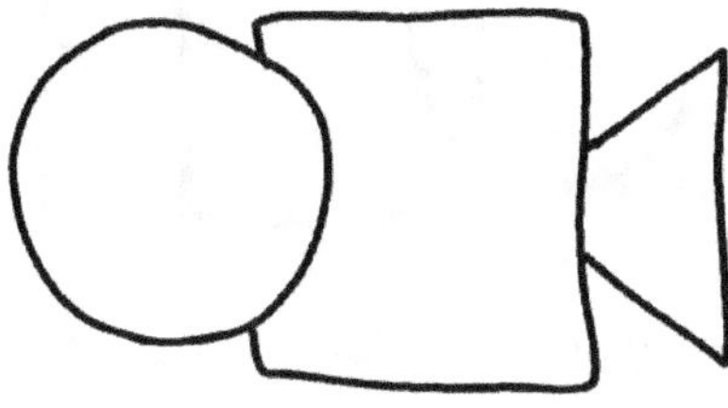

How do you ink a crowd? It's actually just the front-to-back steps all over again...

Follow along with these shapes...

First draw the three shapes with light lines (the lines can overlap and look messy)...

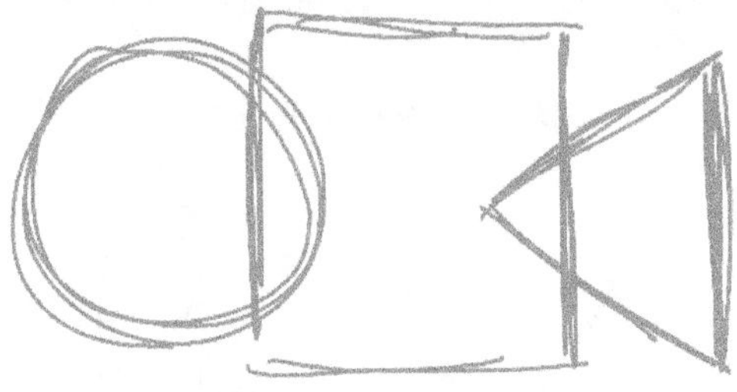

We want the circle to be closest so we ink
that first.

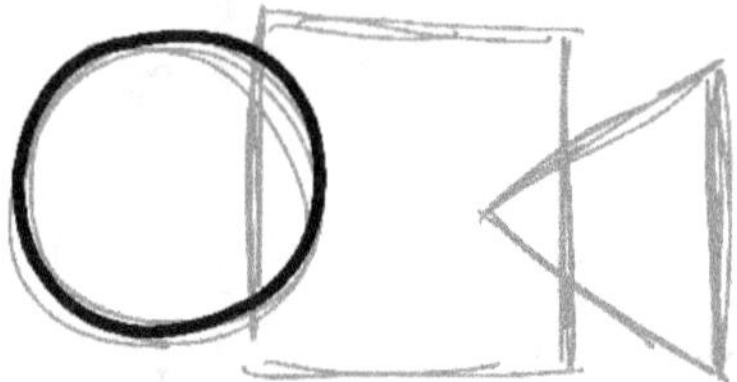

The square is next so we ink that except for
the bit that the circle is covering…

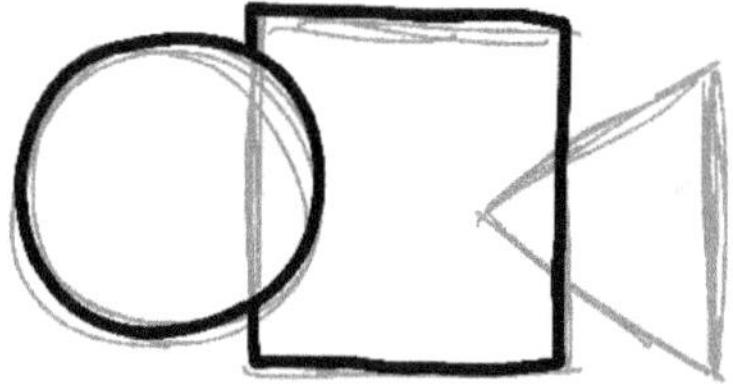

And the triangle is at the back so we ink that
except for the bit that the square is covering.

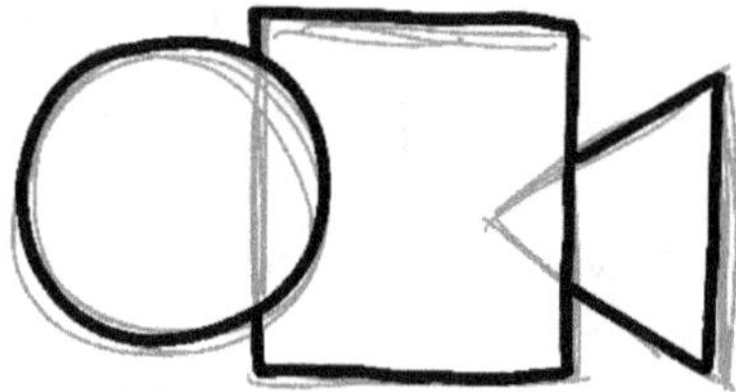

Rub out the light pencil lines and then you'll
have a nice clear picture with layers…

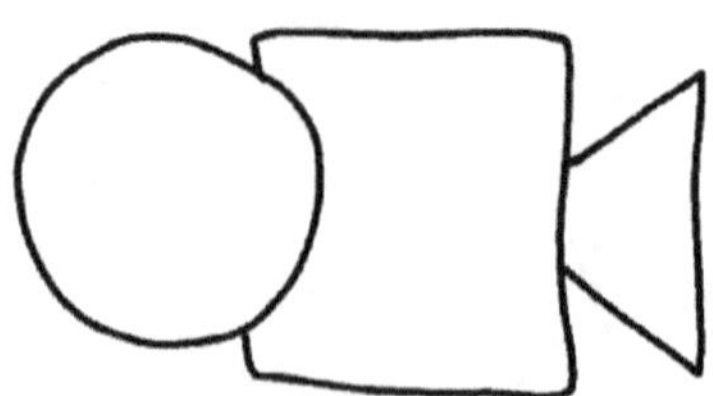

Let's look at how to draw and ink a crowd picture with more complicated stuff like this dinosaur, tree and mountains in the back.

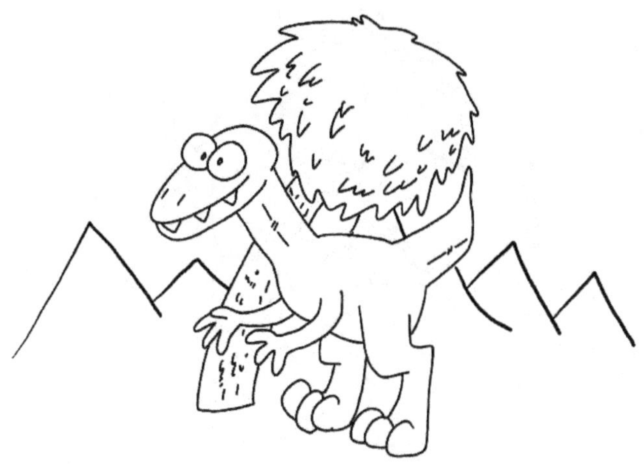

First we draw it all out with light lines, there should be lots of overlapping and mess!

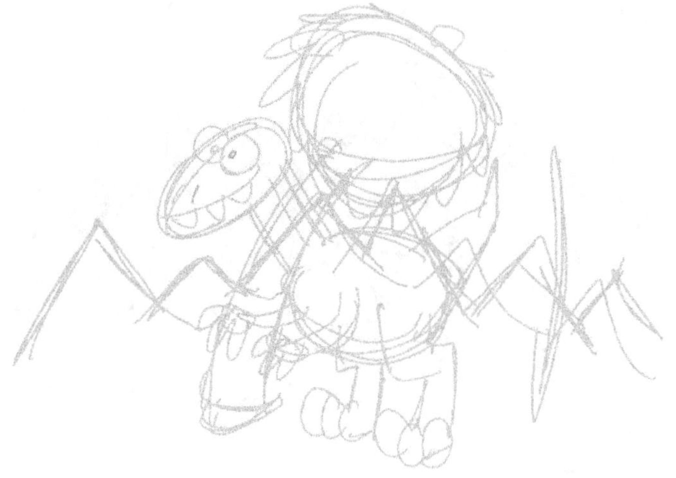

You know what to do next. You ink the closest thing in the crowd (the dinosaur).

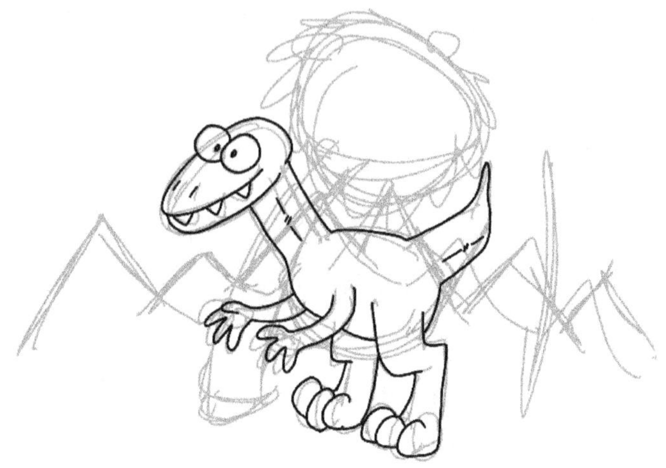

Next ink the next closest thing (the tree) except for the bits the dinosaur is covering.

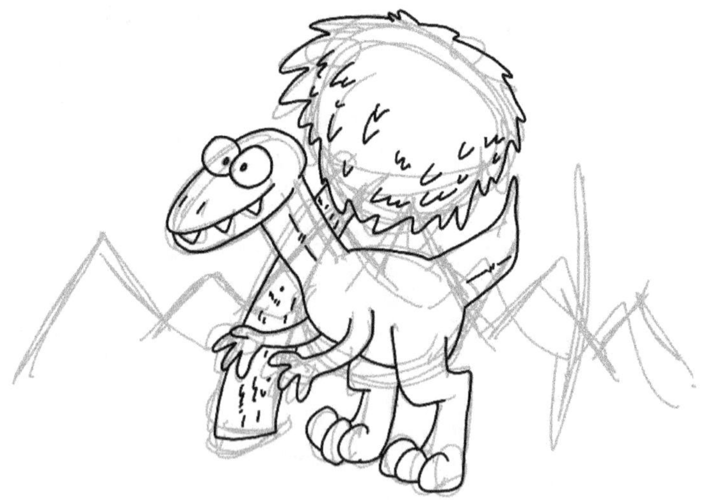

Finally ink the furthest thing away (the mountains) except for the bits covered by the dinosaur and the tree.

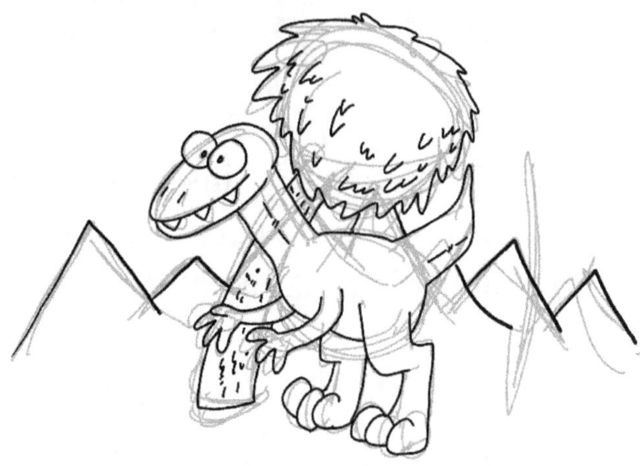

Finally you just have rub out all the light lines and your picture is done!

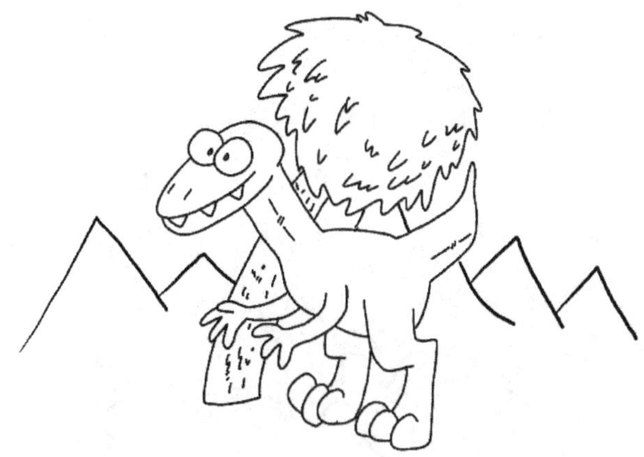

Challenge:

Create your own crowd picture with details and texture and three layers overlapping.

Extra Outlines

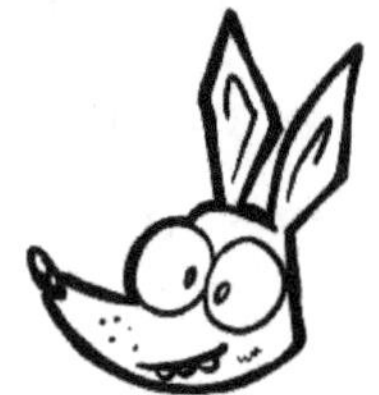

Once you've completely inked something you can give it one more ink line but only on the most outward lines. Like this:

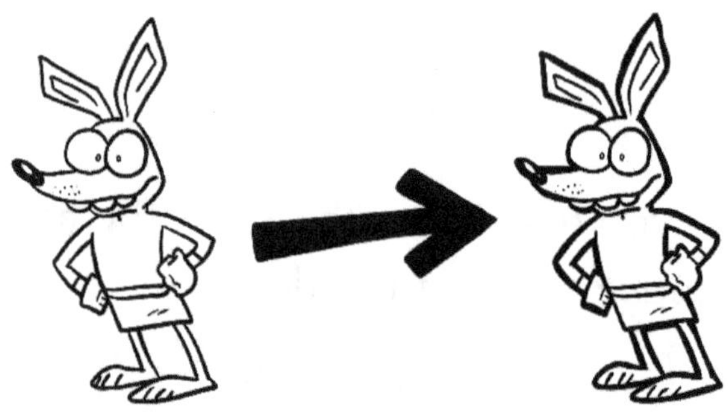

This extra outline makes your picture stand out in a crowd. Have a look at this crowd of Egyptian gods. Nobody really stands out yet.

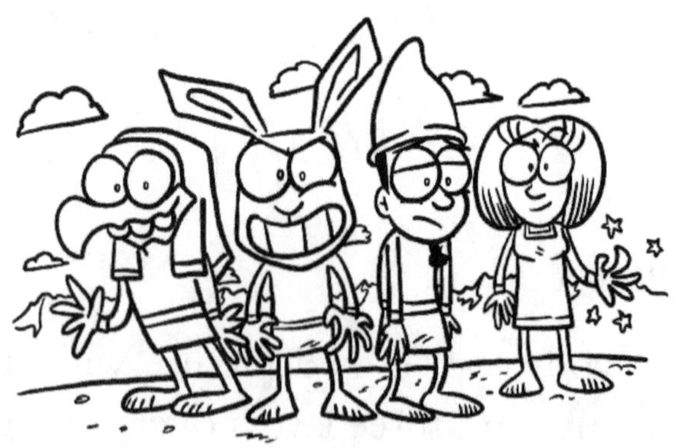

But if we add an outline to one character, they stand out even in a crowd…

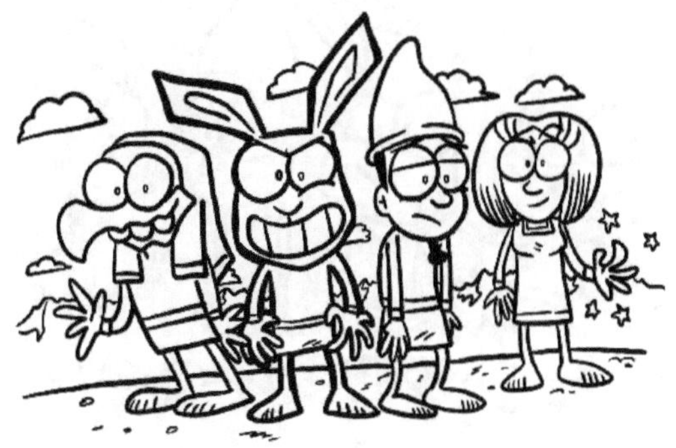

See how outlining different characters takes your attention? Like this…

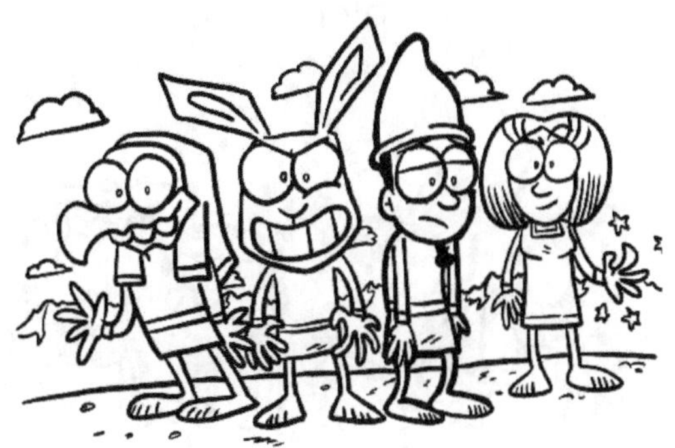

Or this…

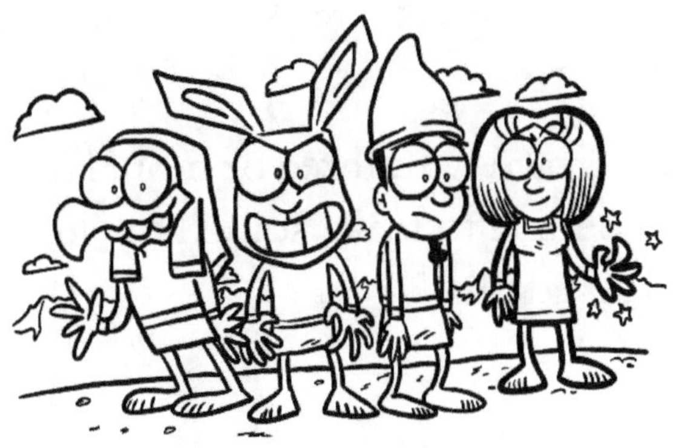

And this, too…

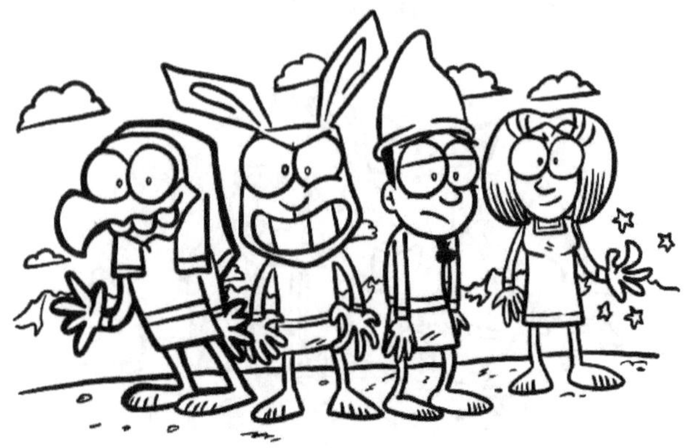

You can also use an outline on all the characters in the crowd if you want everyone to stand out in the picture…

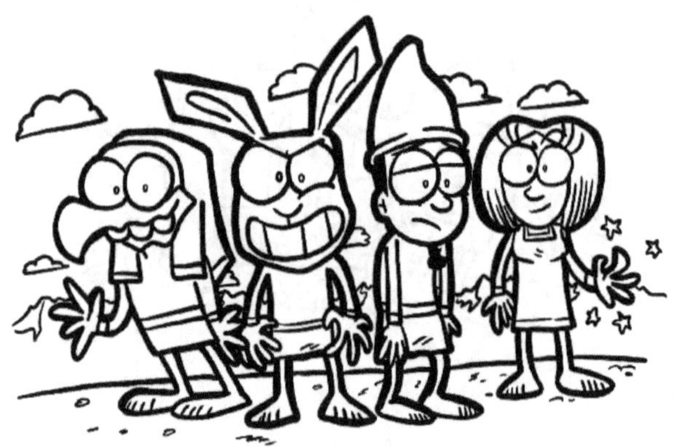

Challenge:

Draw a crowd with three or more layers and add an outline to make something in the crowd stand out.

WARNING

All the stuff we looked at is called 'Basic Stuff' but that doesn't mean it's easy!

No there's a lot of hard stuff you've just covered.

And it's really important too!

So, before you move on to the rest of the book make sure you are really, really confident to use all of the stuff we just looked at.

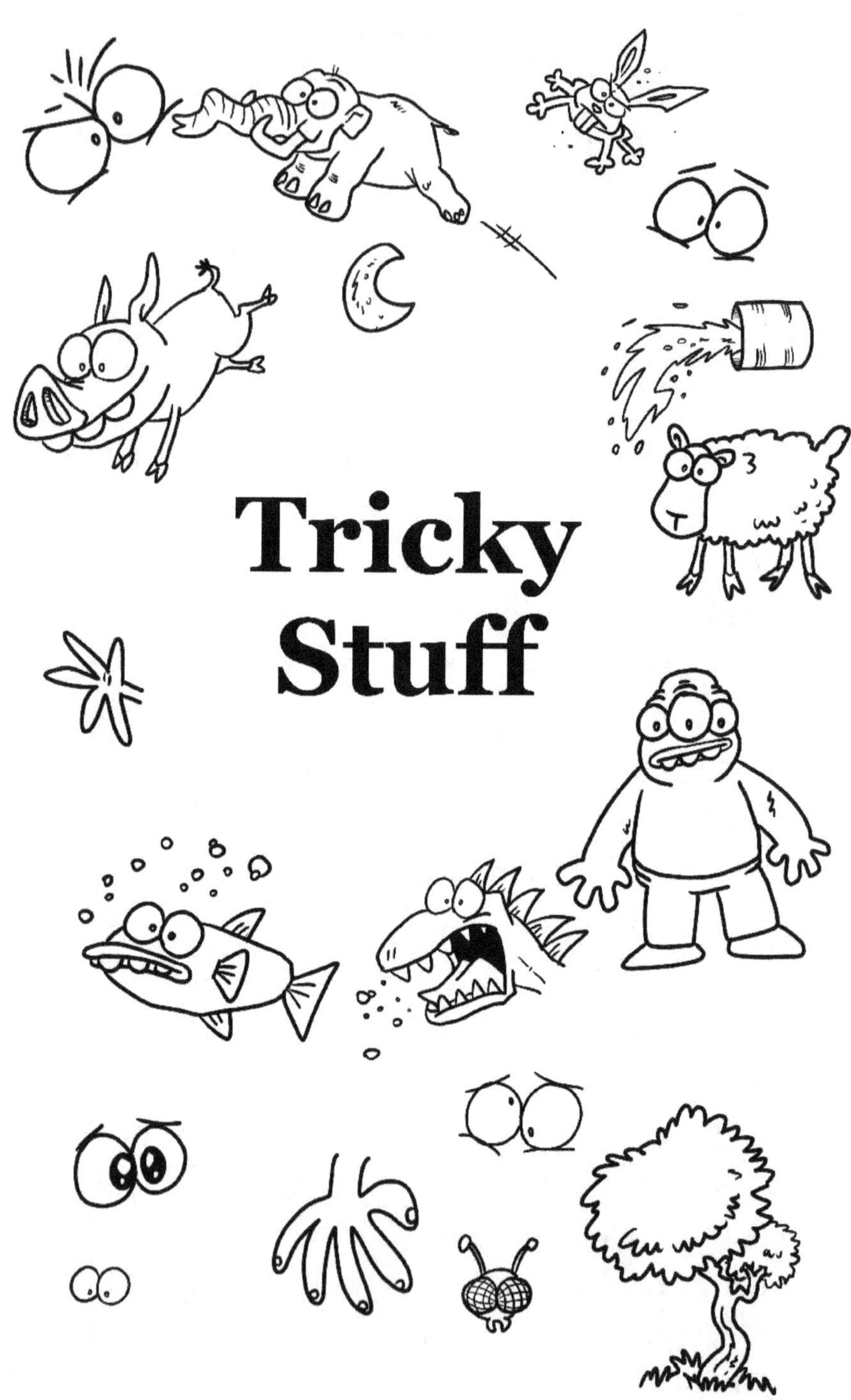

Tricky Stuff

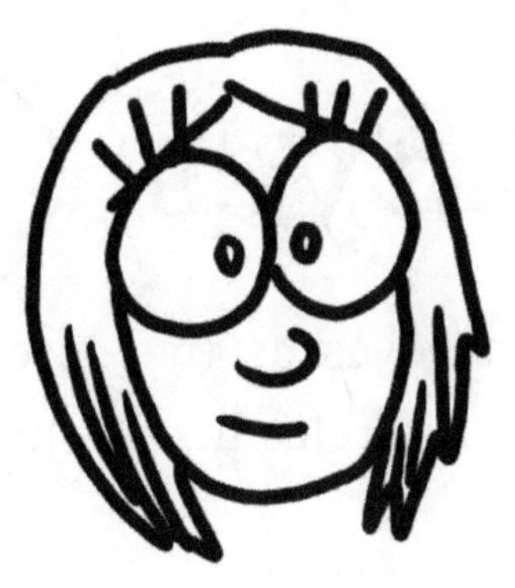

People Stuff

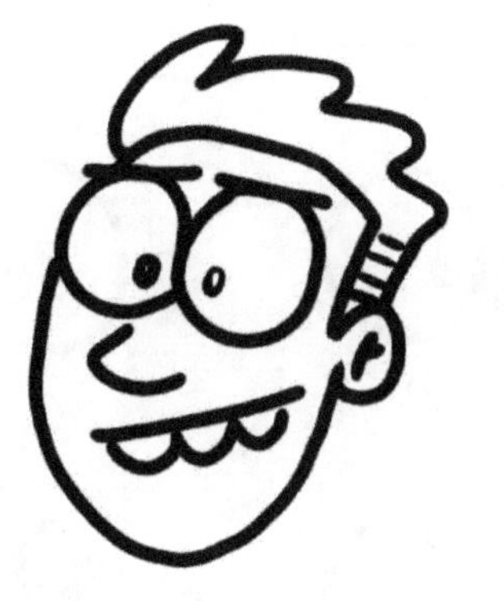

Eyes

I draw all my eyes as two circles with two smaller dots or circles inside them like this:

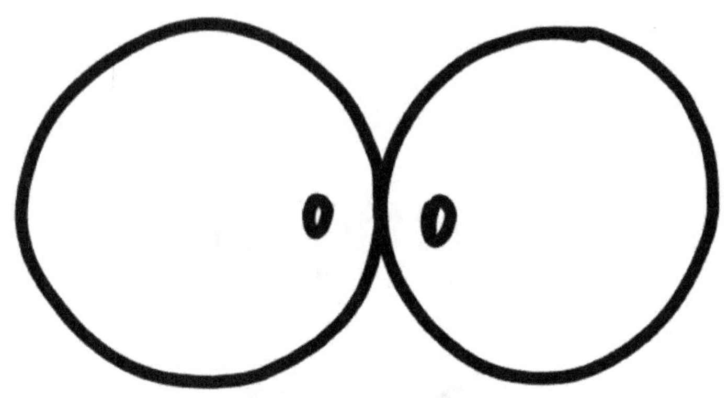

You can change the characters of eyes by changing the circles or dots in the eyes.

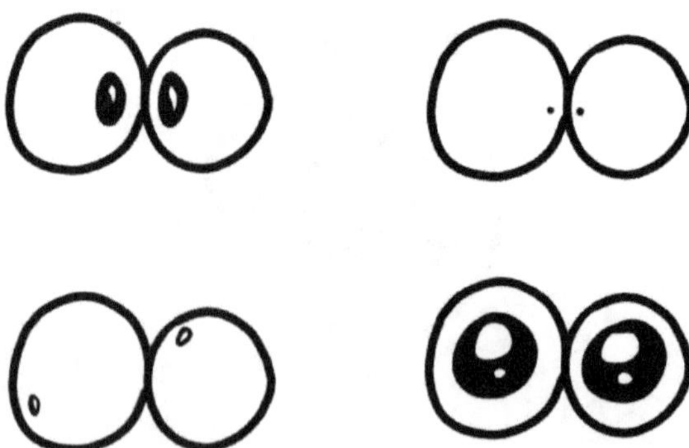

To give the eyes some character and make
them interesting I add lines like these:

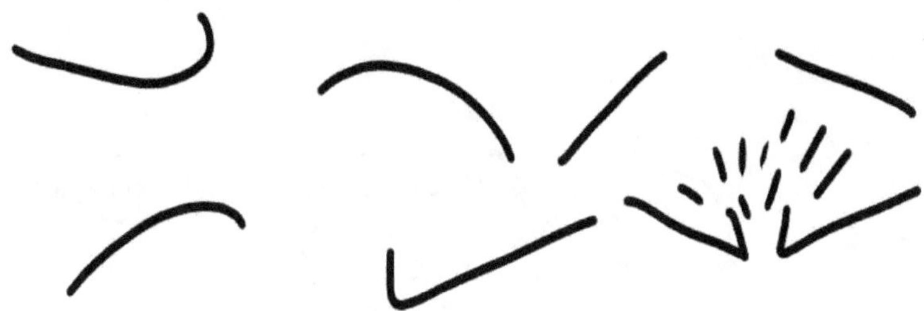

Here's what some lines at the top of the
eyes can do:

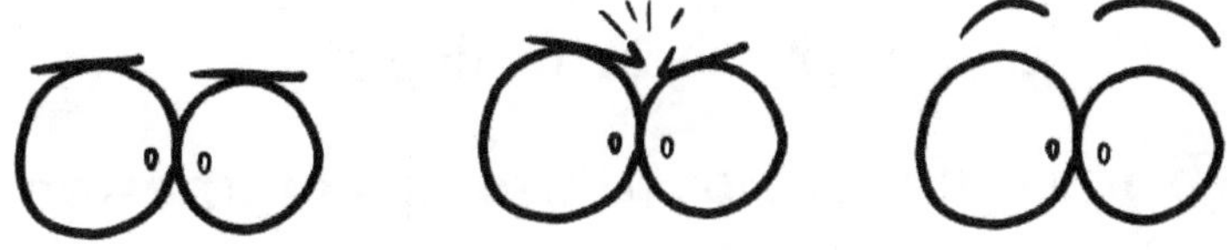

You can add lines to the bottom of eyes, too.
Like this:

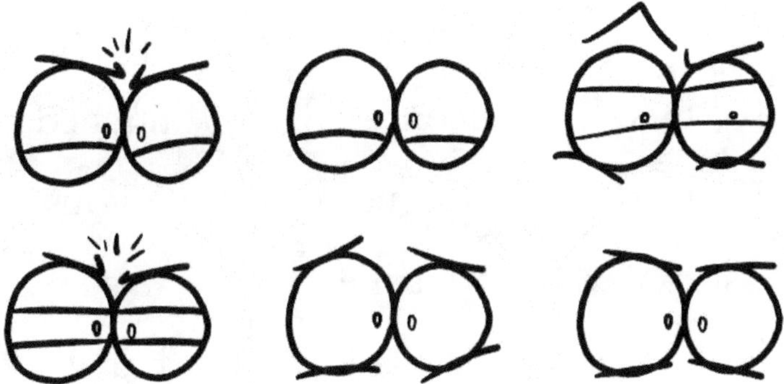

Eyes tell you all about how a character is feeling. All you can see are these eyes but you know exactly how these characters are feeling:

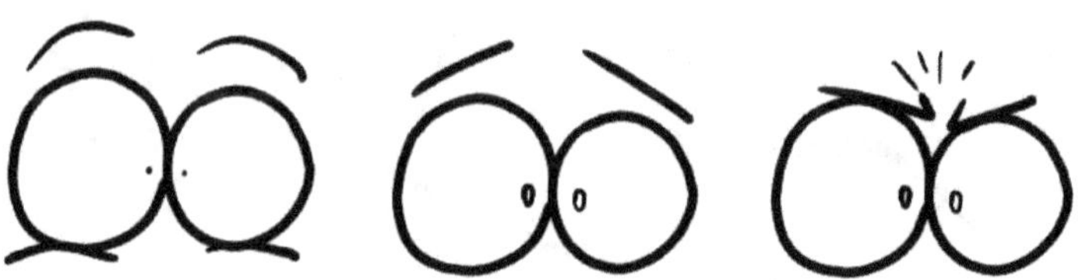

Challenge:

Use eyes to show these feelings:

(Bonus tip: try not to use lots of lines on your eyes. Less lines are better.)

angry	bored	happy
proud	sad	lost
scared	furious	suspicious
tired	confused	outraged
mad	disgusted	nervous
surprised	terrified	rage
in love	hate	brave
serious	calm	goof

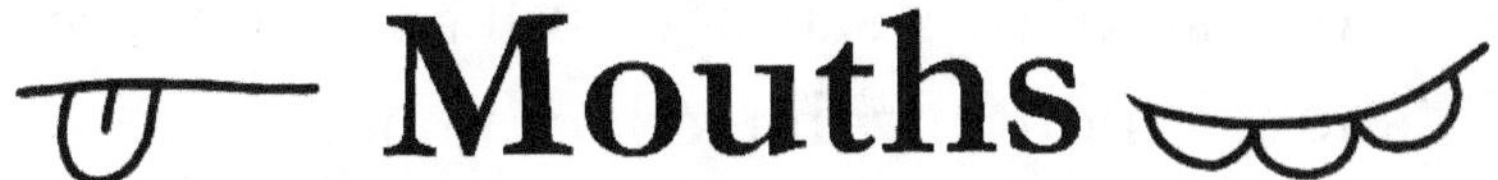# Mouths

A mouth can be a line. It can be straight, tilted or curved. These are all mouths:

You can stick some teeth out of it.

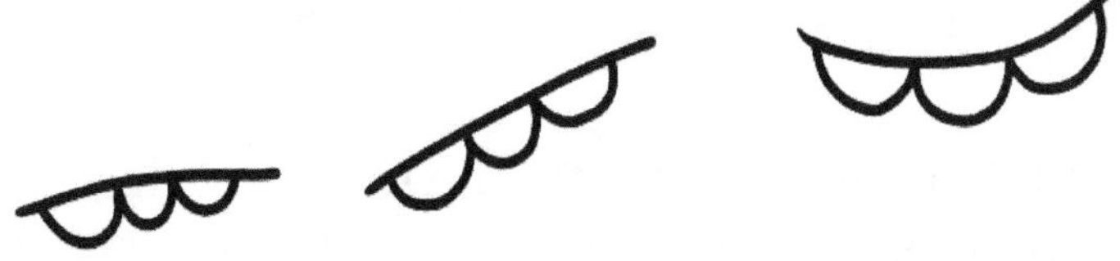

Or a tongue.

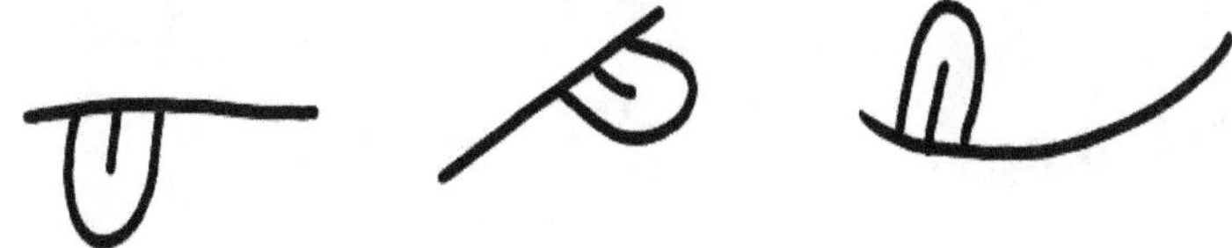

You can draw a sausage with some lines to show a mouth with teeth clenched.

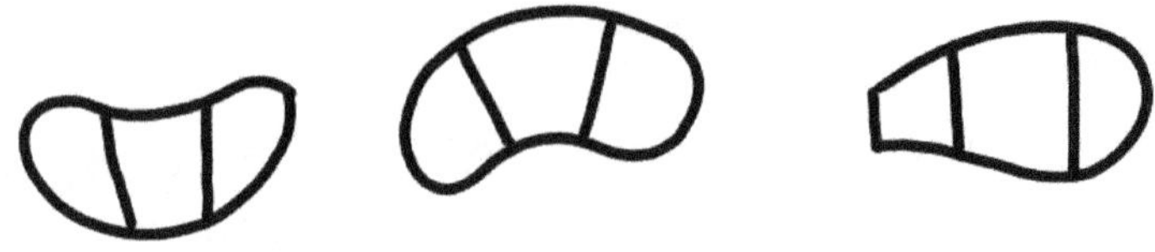

You can open the mouth a little or a lot.

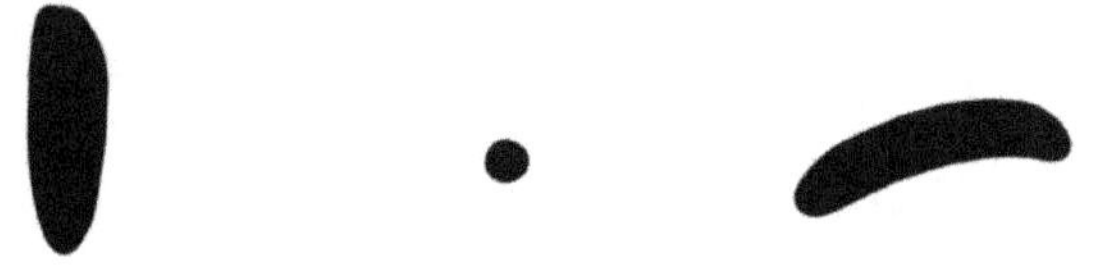

You can sneak some teeth or tongue in there, too.

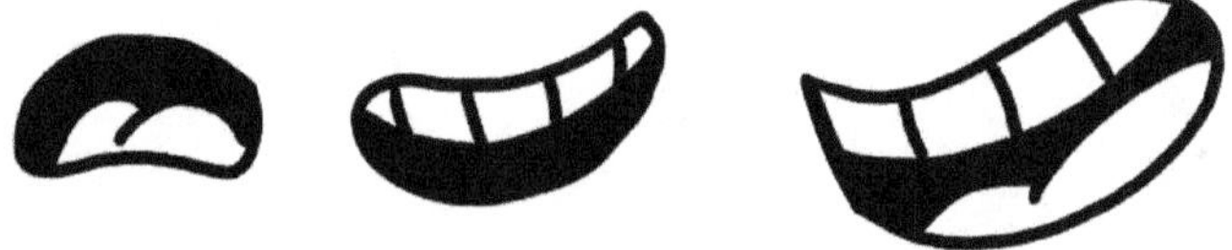

Challenge:

How many different mouths can you make?

Think of all the emotions you can show with just a mouth.

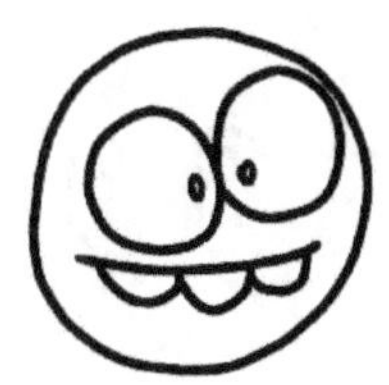 # Eyes and Mouths 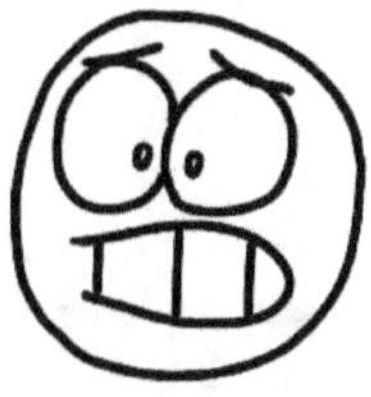

The mouth and eyes tell nearly everything about who a character is. Look:

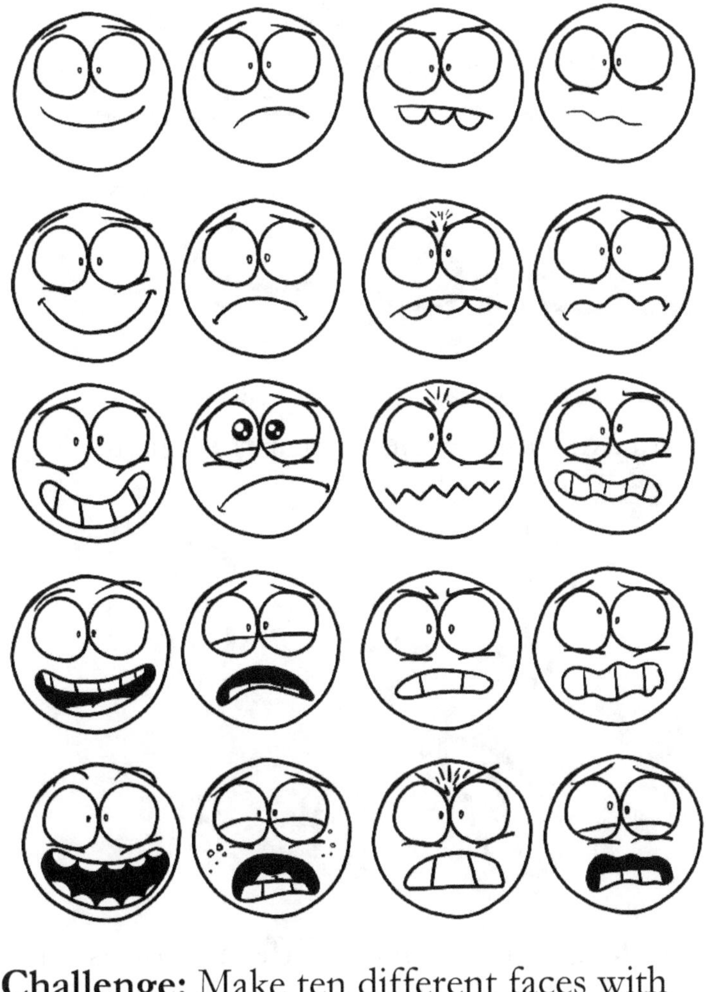

Challenge: Make ten different faces with just the eyes and a mouth.

Noses and Ears

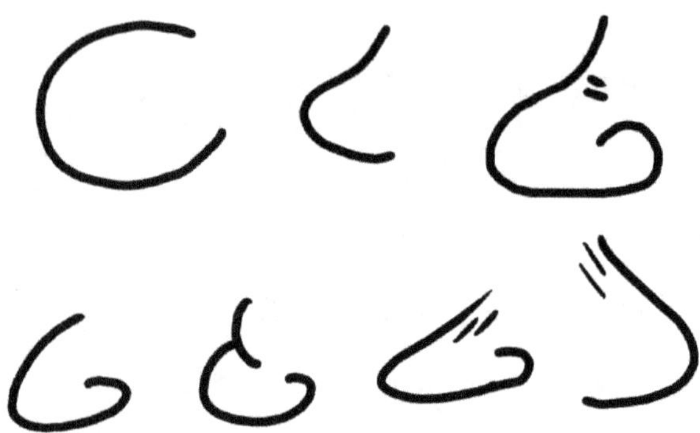

A nose can just be a line or a few lines:

And so can an ear. You just have to add some extra lines inside the ear for the ear hole:

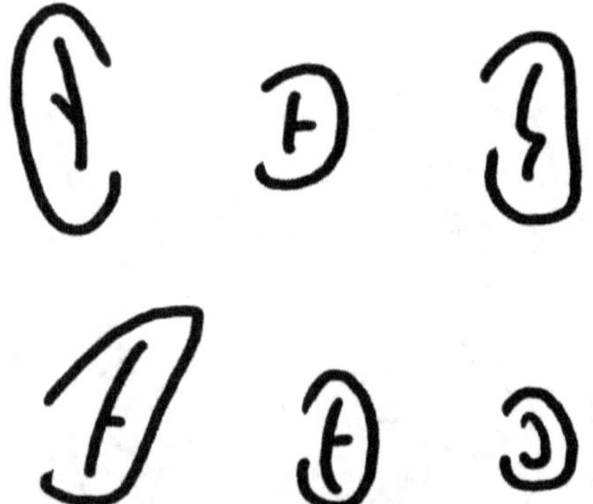

Challenge: How many different noses and ears can you draw?

Hair

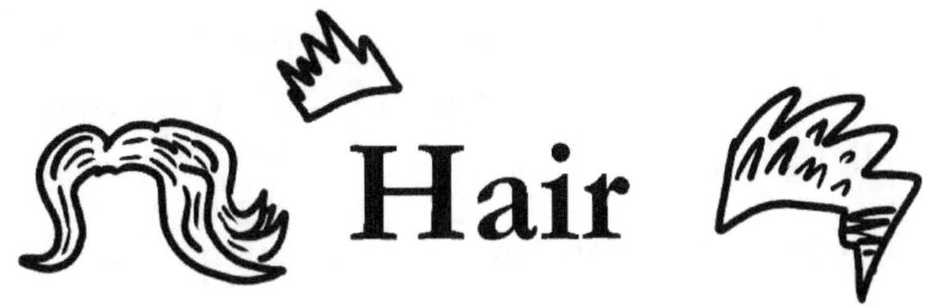

You can add hair once everything else is done on the head. Like this:

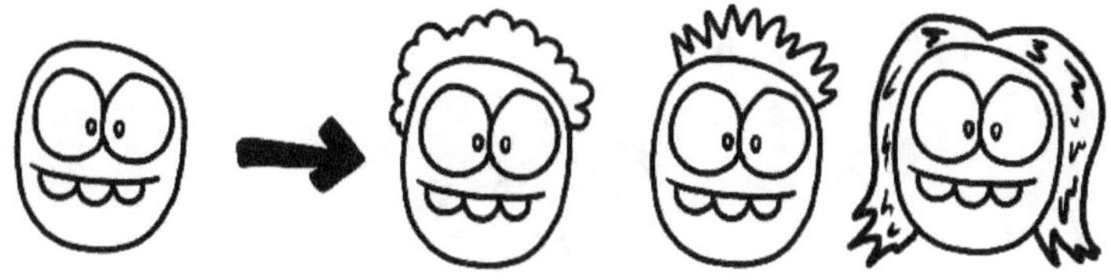

Or you can plan for the hair to cover part of the face like this:

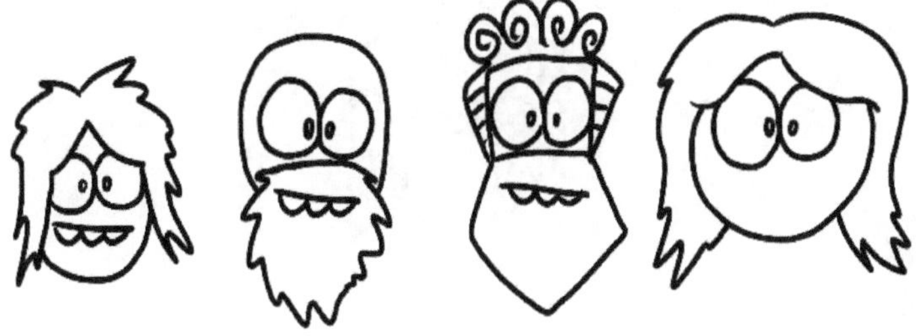

And if you want to draw hair that covers part of the face you first have to plan the hair in light lines.

Here is my plan for a bearded hairy face:

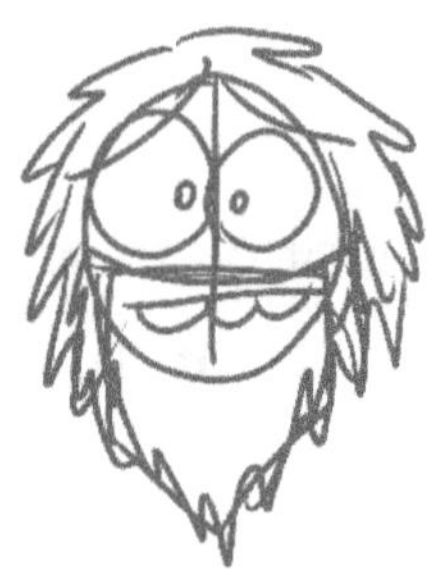

Here are my inks:

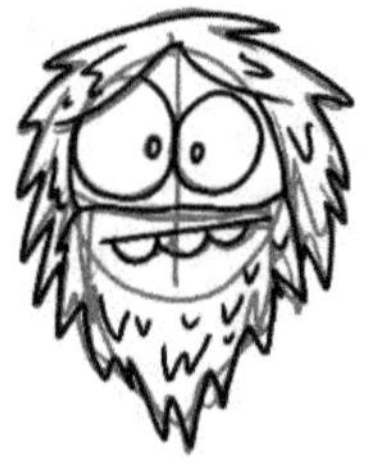

And after I rub out the light lines, this is how it looks:

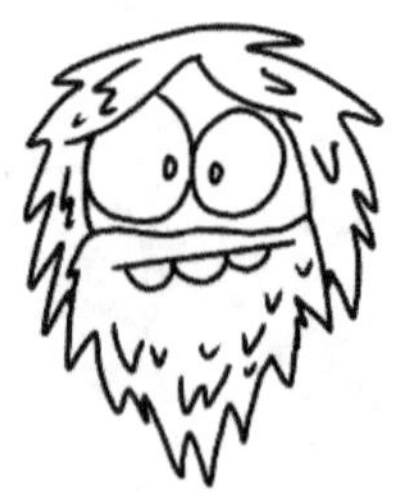

Challenge:

Make ten different hair styles.

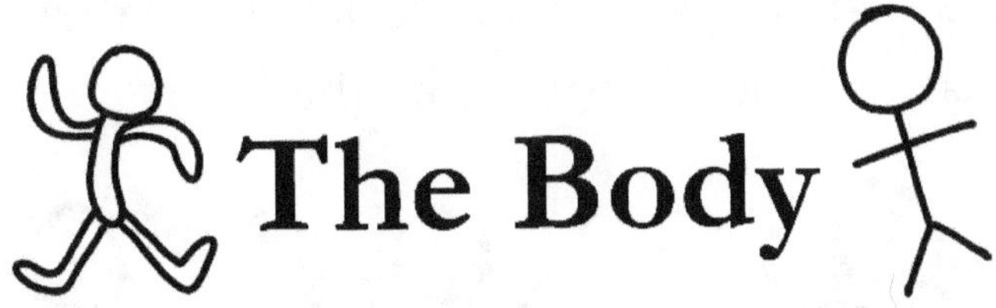

The Body

If you're stuck drawing bodies like this stick person…

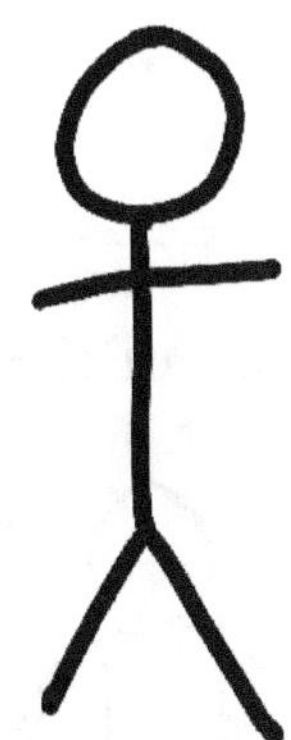

Try drawing the stick arms and legs bendy instead of straight. Like this…

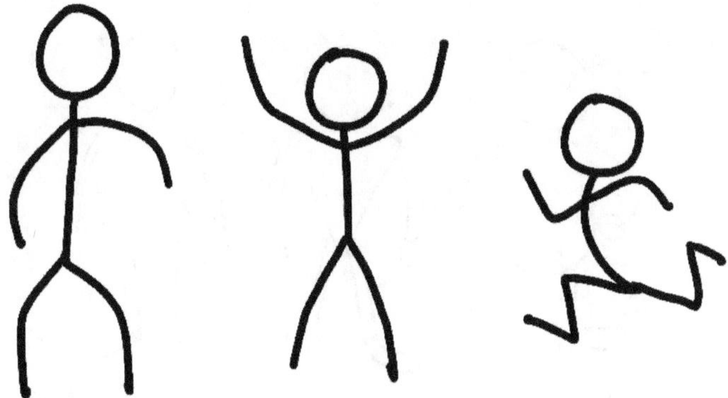

And instead of a stick torso, give them a square-ish bendy torso like this…

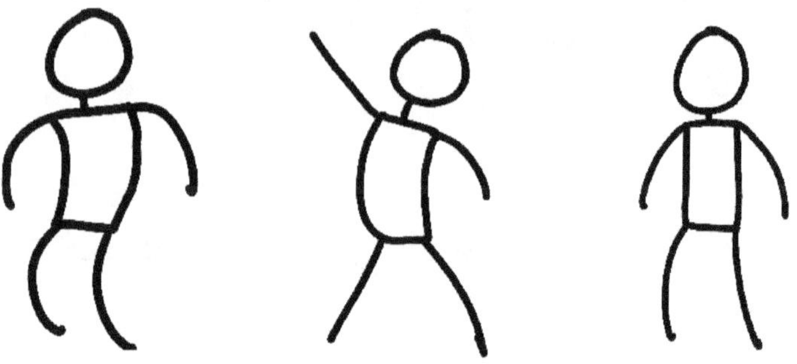

Then make the bendy arms and legs into sausages with blobs on the end like this…

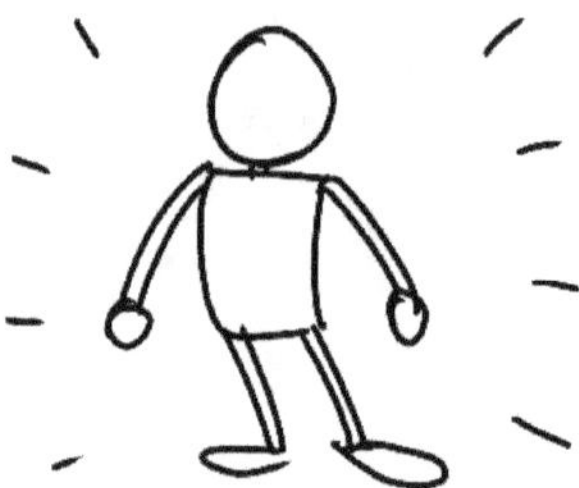

The torso doesn't just have to be square-ish. It can be all sorts of shapes.

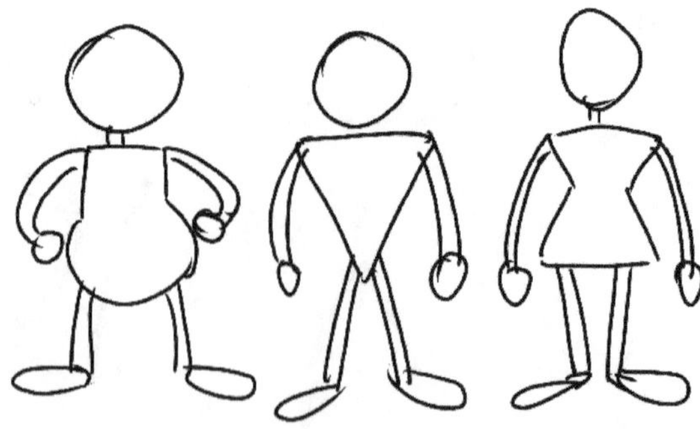

Look at these different bodies. You know what they're doing because of how the torso and limbs fit together.

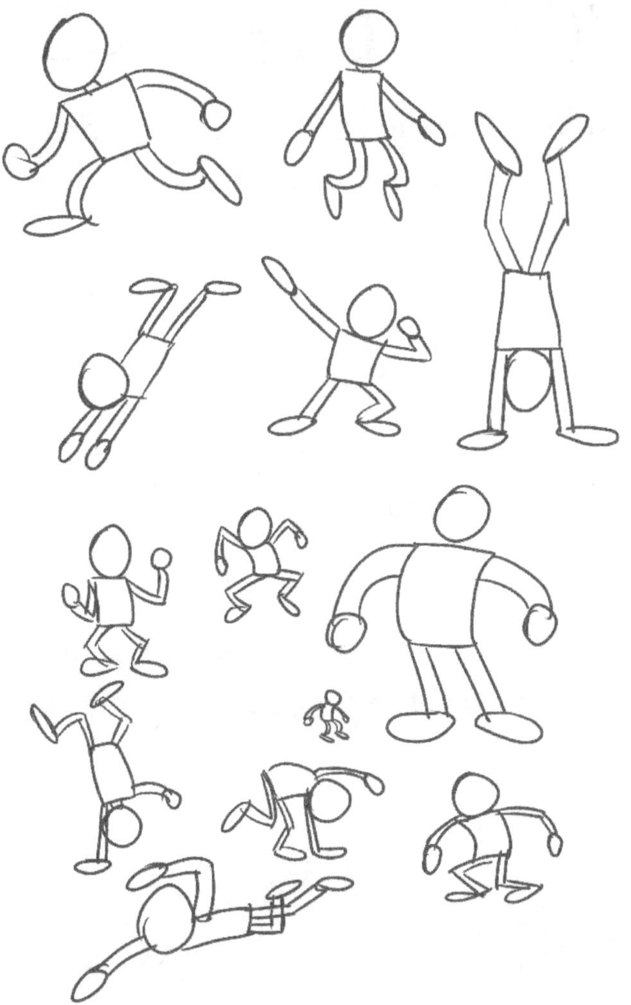

Challenge:

Let's see you draw ten different bodies doing ten different things!

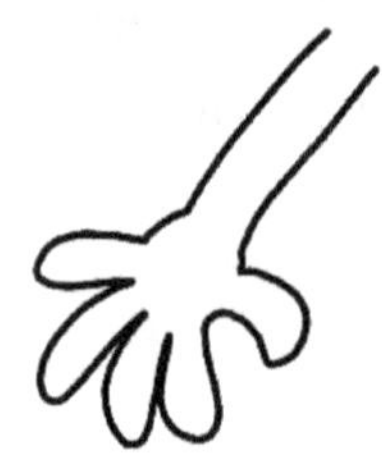

Hands
and
Feet

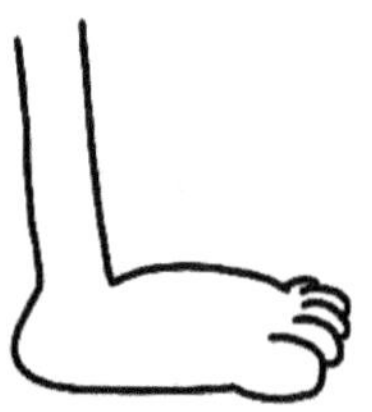

To draw the hand start with the arm and a
circle where the hand will be…

Add five sausages all curving one way for
the fingers and the other way for the thumb.

Ink it, erase the light lines and you've got a hand.

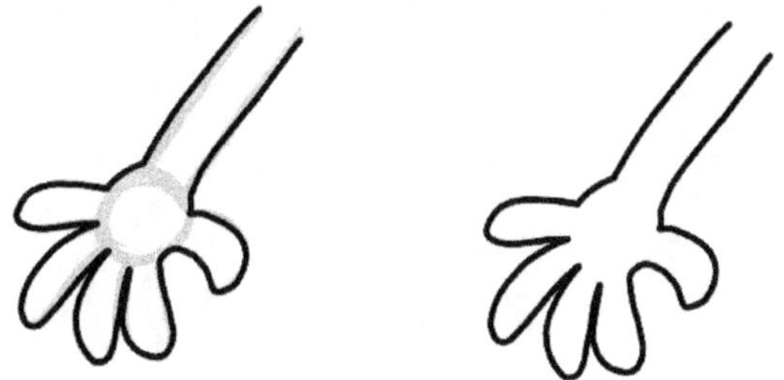

You can make the fingers and thumb thicker or thinner too…

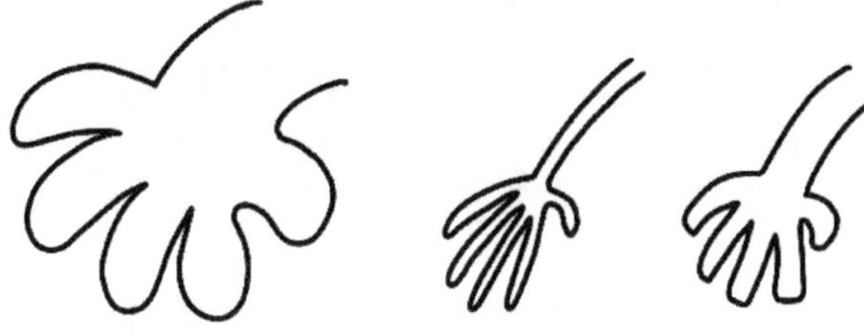

Challenge:

Draw a hand doing ten different things.

Here are some ideas:

Holding something that is heavy.

Holding something that is light.

Making a fist.

Pointing.

Giving a thumbs up.

To draw a foot, draw the leg then add a sausage where the foot goes. You can then add lines to show where the toes are…

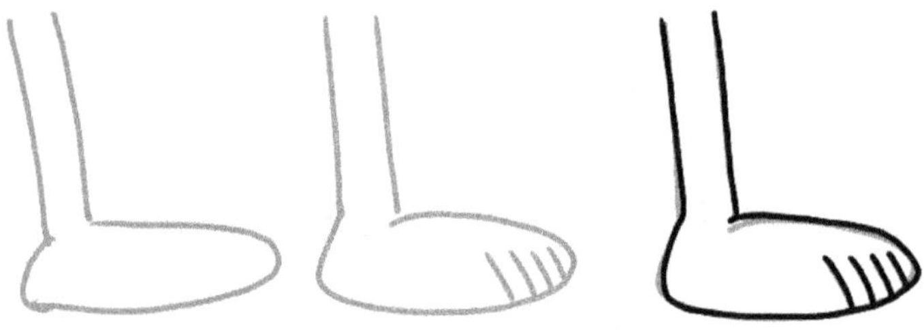

Or you can add five mini sausages for the toes. Ink them, erase the light lines and you've got feet.

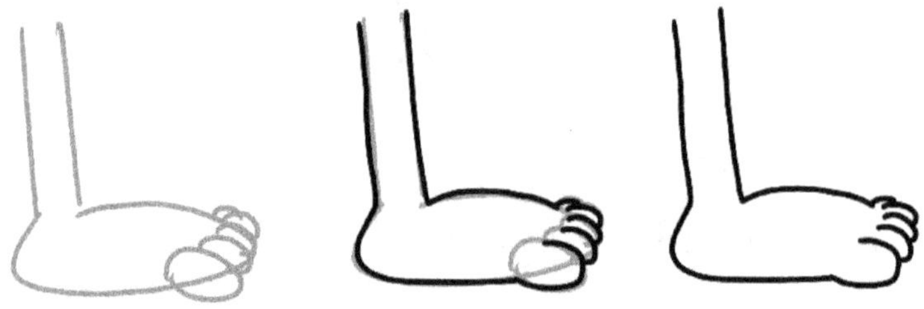

Challenge:

How many different types of feet can you make?

Create ten different hands or feet. They could be younger, older, strong or not so strong…

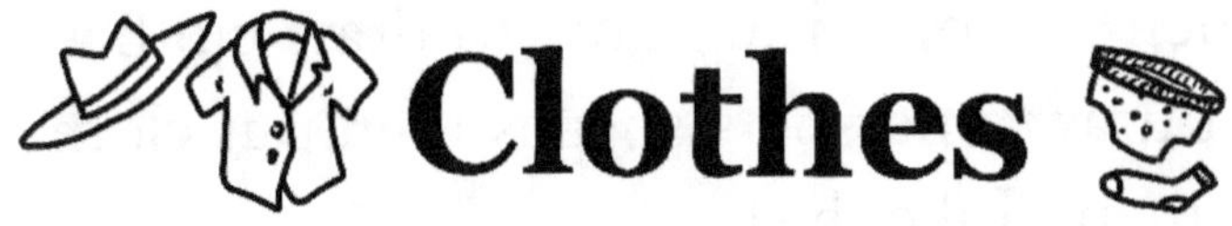

Clothes

One way to draw clothes is to draw lines on a person like this:

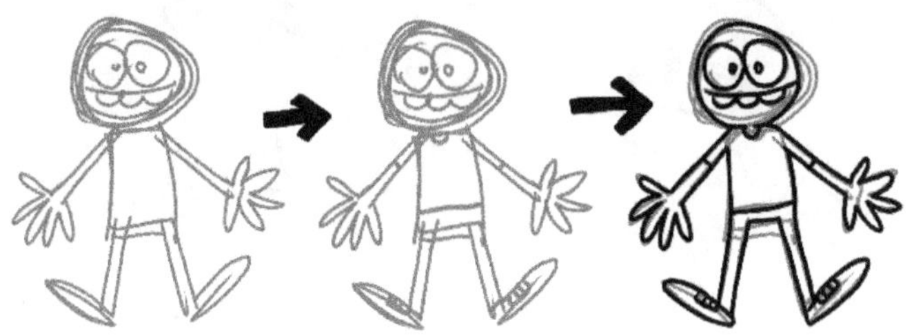

Another way is to draw your person using light lines, then draw the clothes with their own lines over the top of them. Like this:

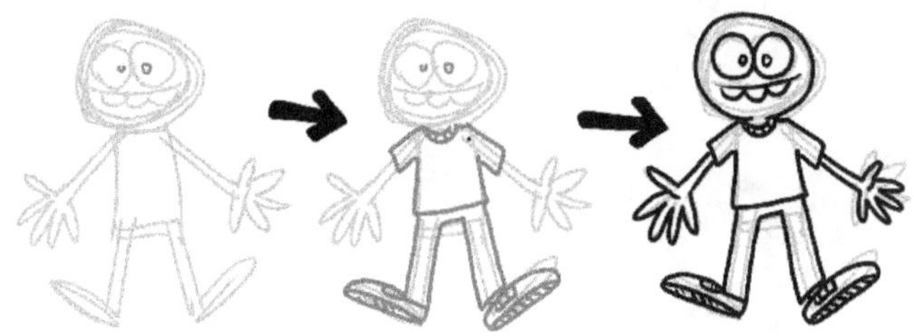

Which do you think looks better? When it's your picture, it's up to you how you draw it.

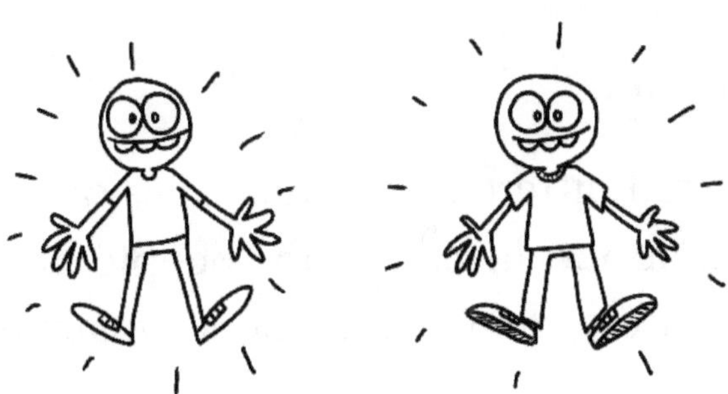

When I'm practising how to draw clothes, I just draw a person's shapes then put clothes on them. Like this:

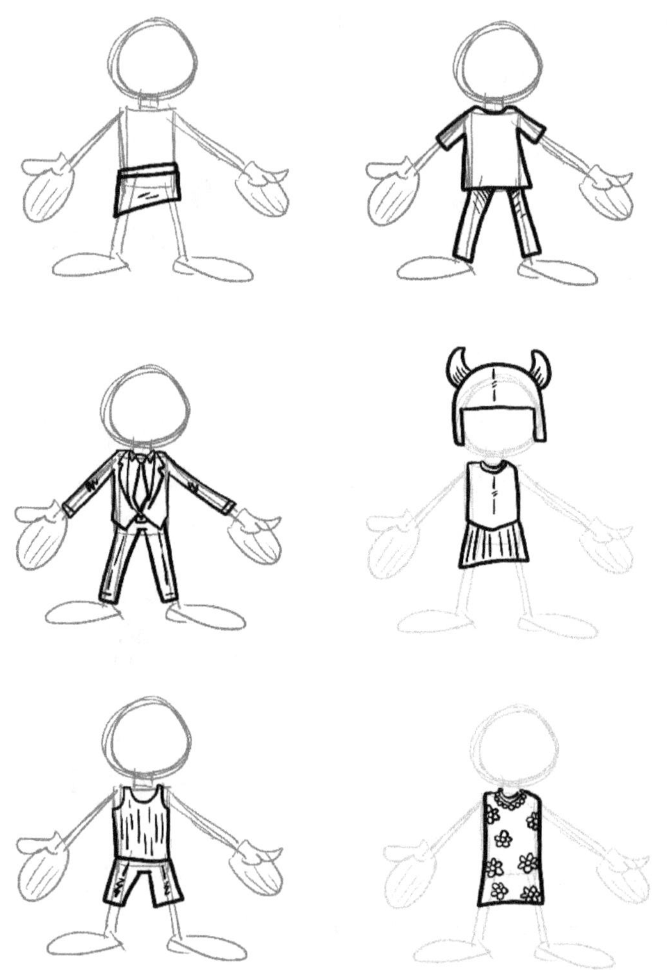

Challenge:

Draw ten different sets of clothes on people. Think about different jobs people have like fire fighters, dentists, teachers, whatever!

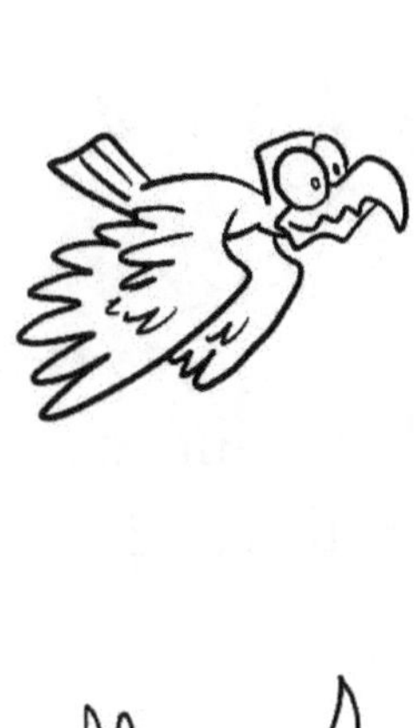

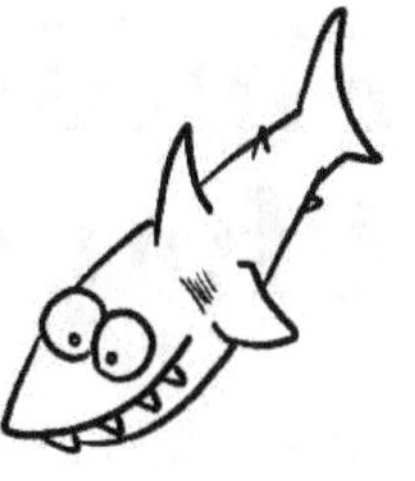

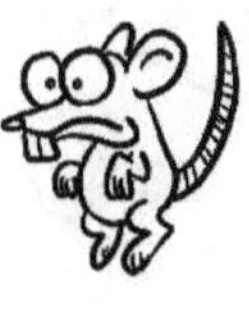

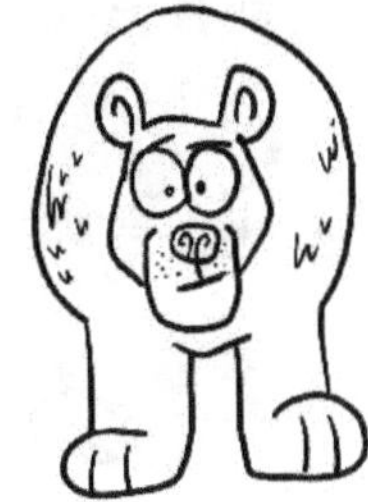

Animal Stuff

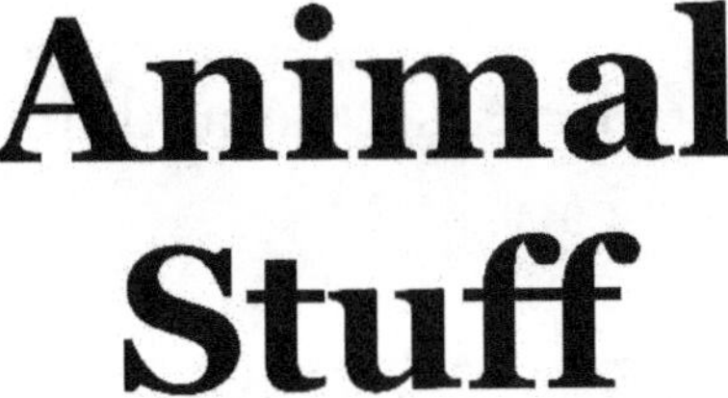

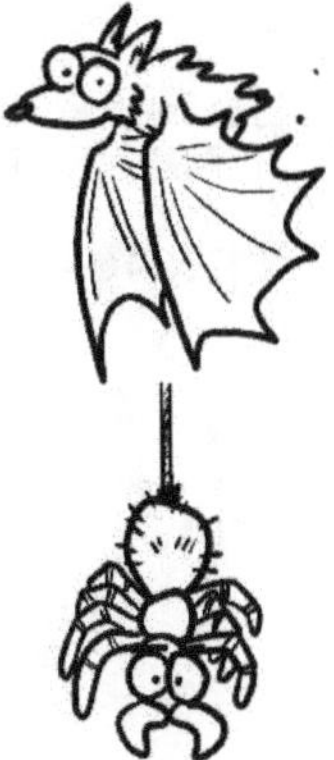

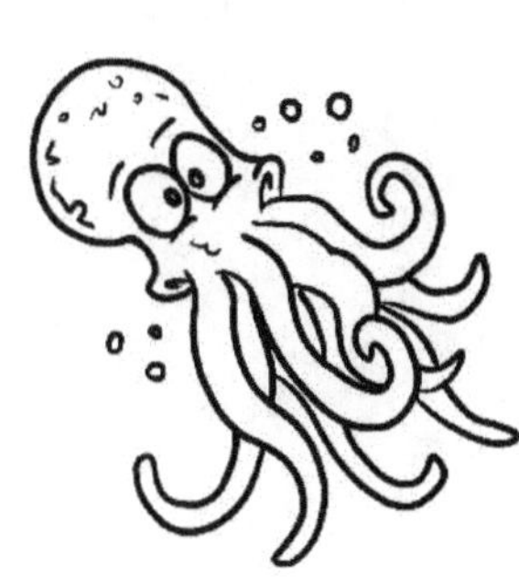

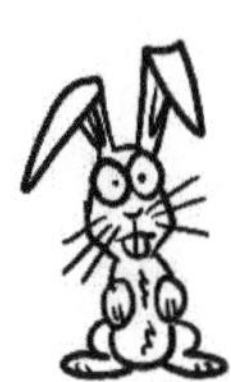

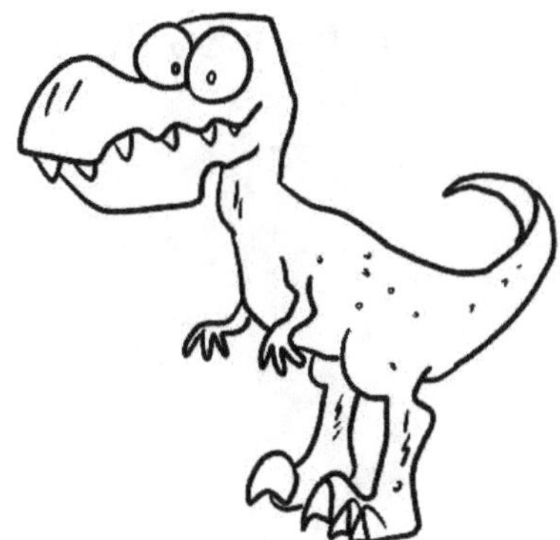

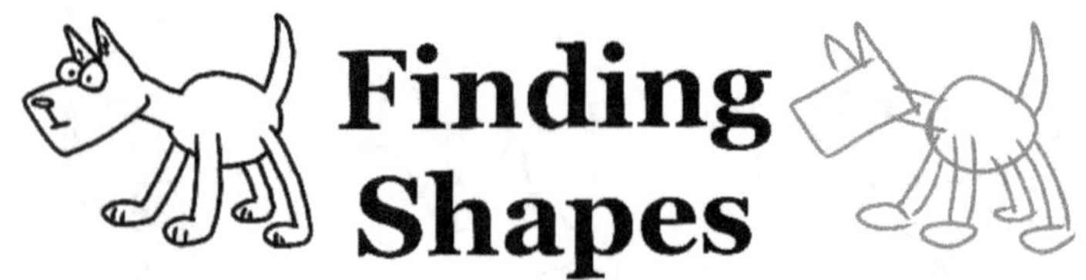

Finding Shapes

For everything else in this book, I want you to look for the shapes in the pictures and figure out how to draw them.

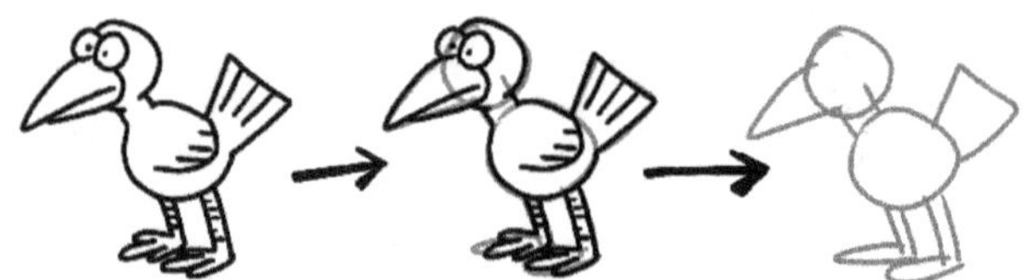

For example, here is a cat and here are the shapes in the cat…

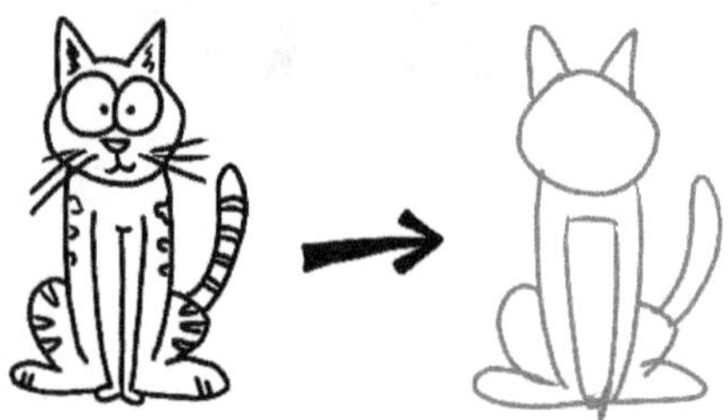

Or, they could look like this or this or this…

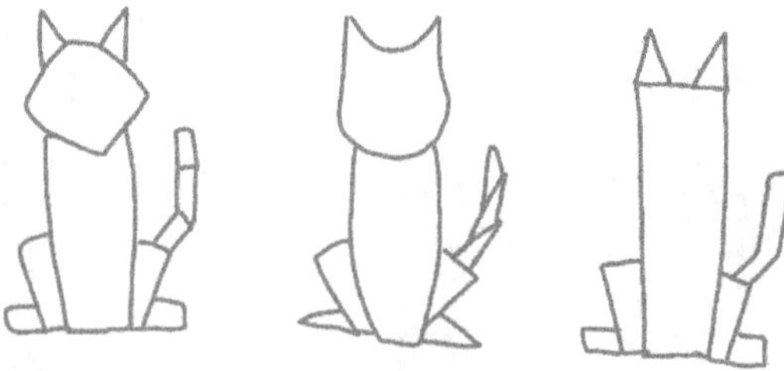

Try drawing the other stuff in this book by finding the shapes and drawing from there.

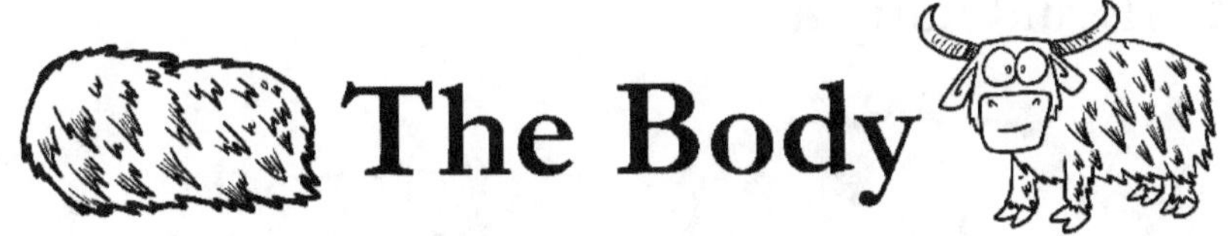

The Body

When I practise what a body is covered with,
I start with a blob like this:

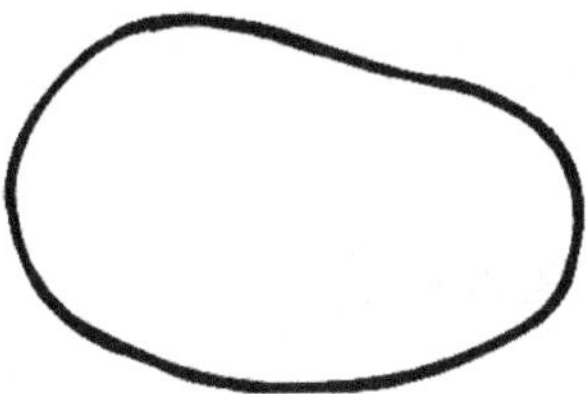

Then I draw stuff on it…

Here's long and wavy fur…

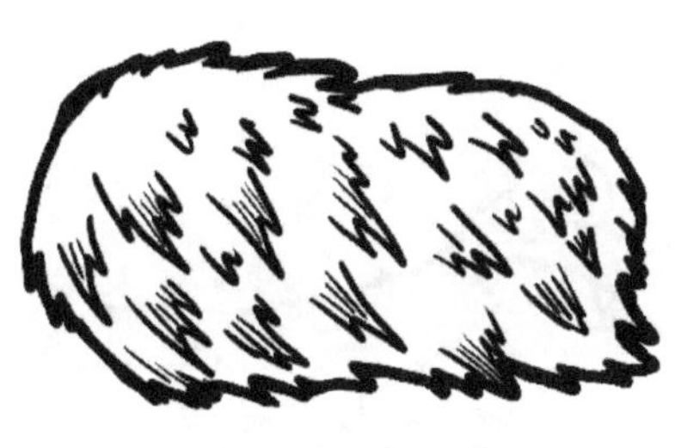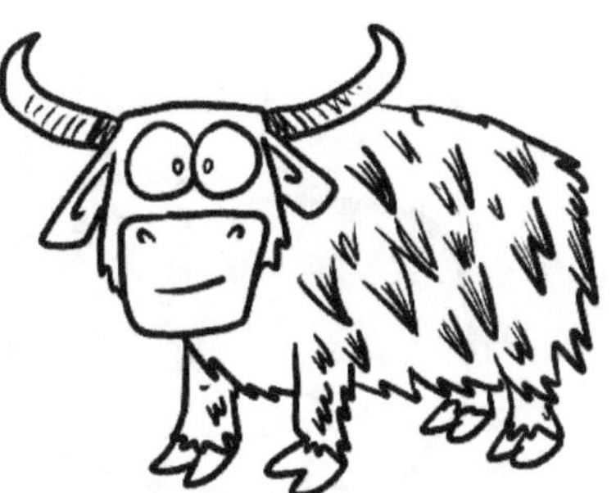

Short and spiky fur…

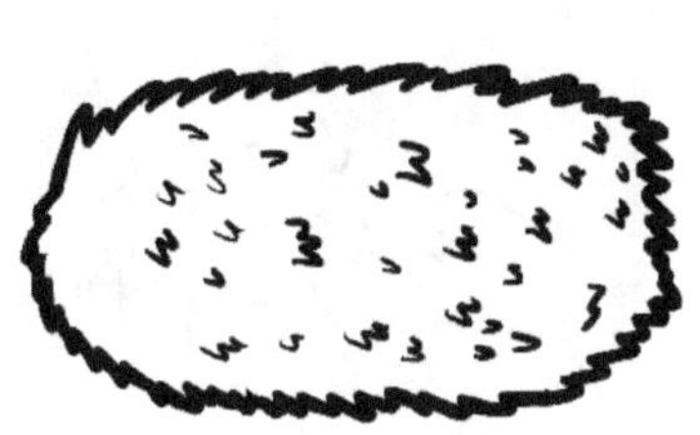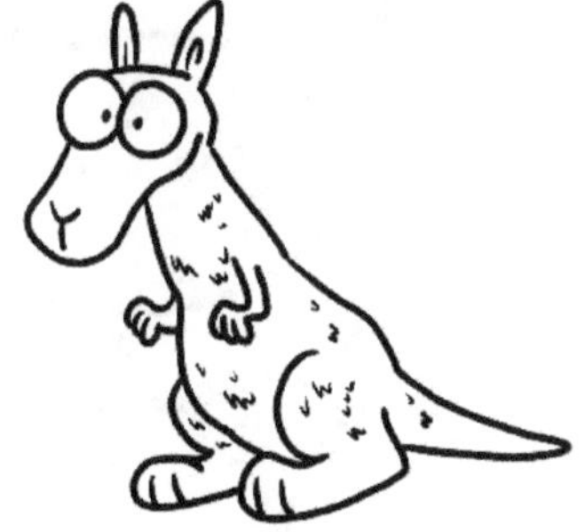

Curly and fluffy fur…

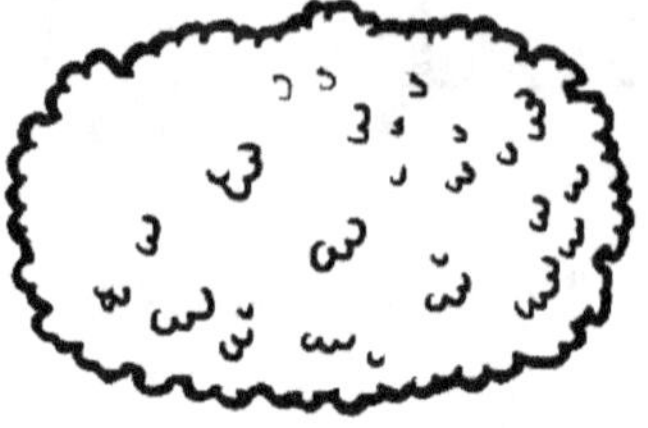 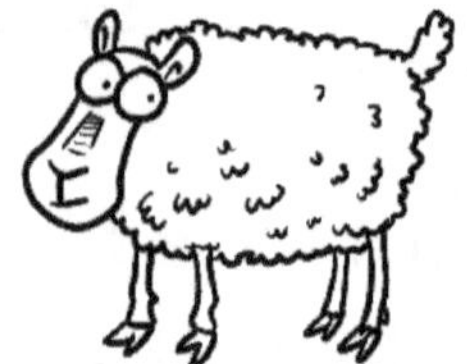

Feathers…

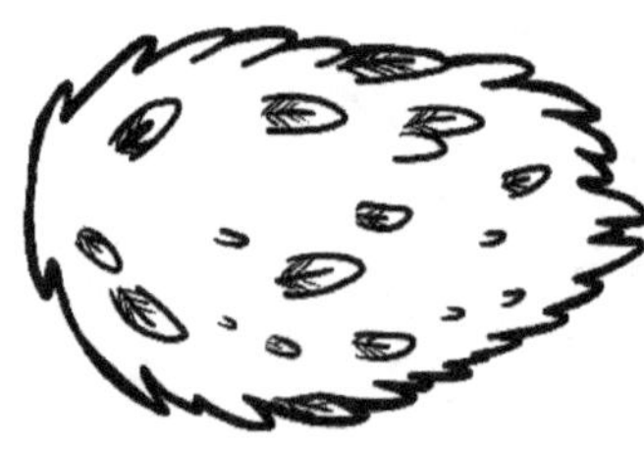 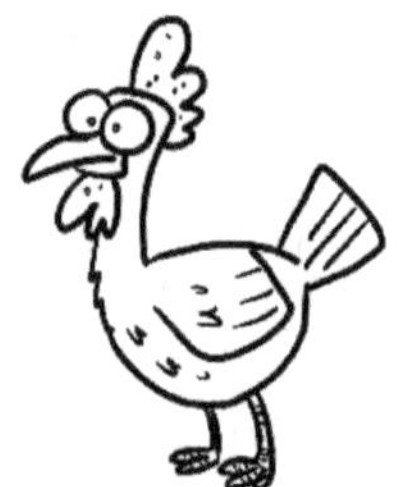

Scales like a fish or reptile…

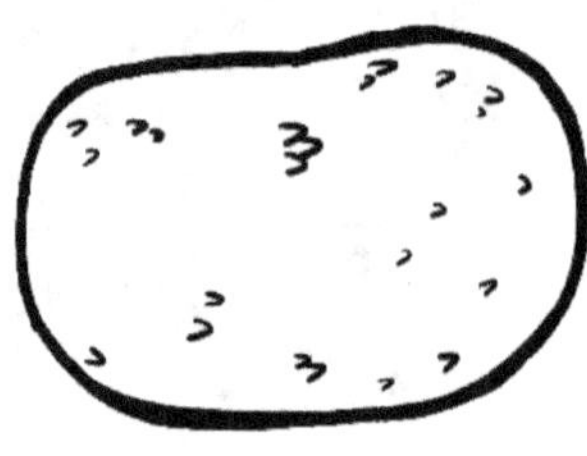 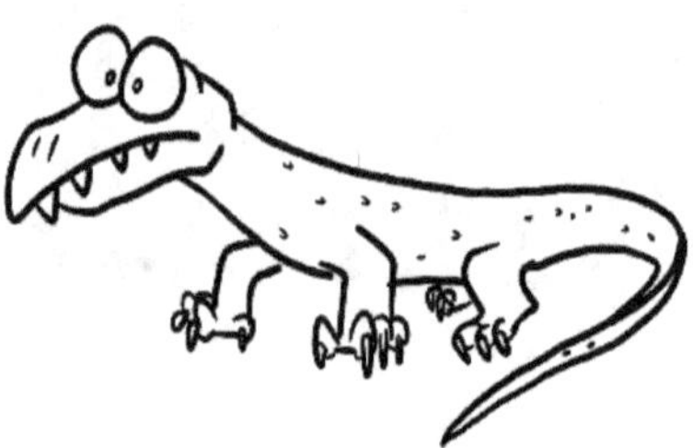

A shell or exoskeleton…

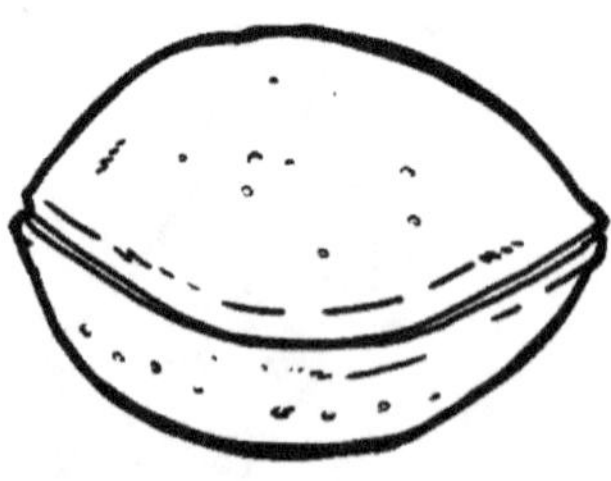 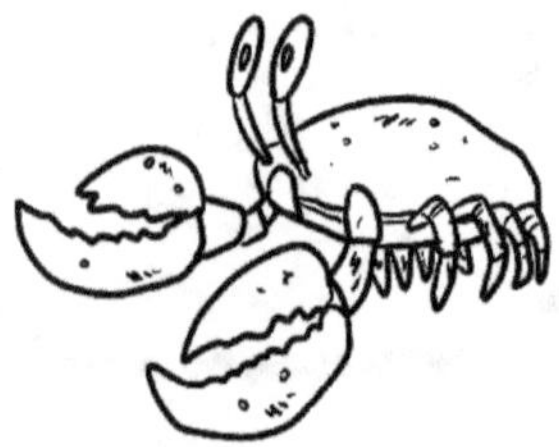

Weird slimy skin…

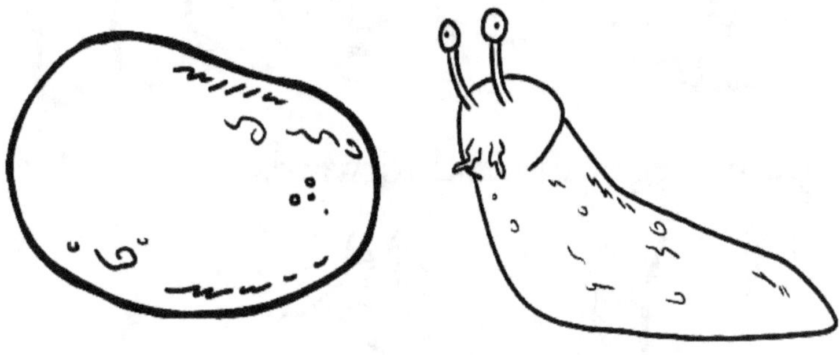

Rough skin like a shark…

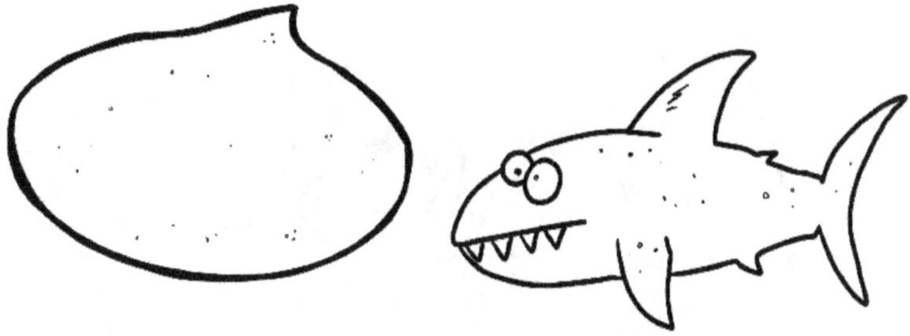

There can also be a mixture of body covers on animal. For example:

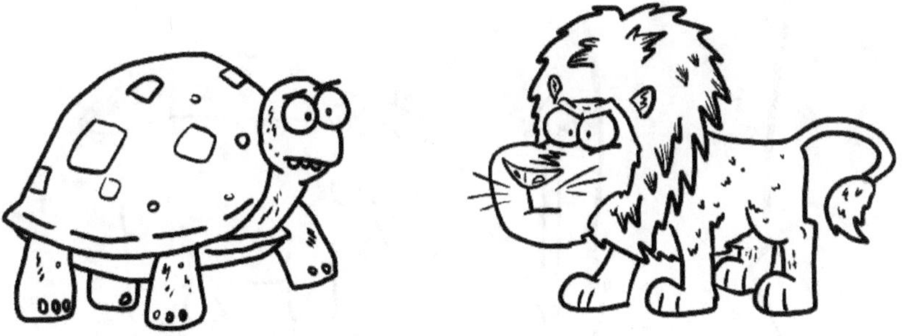

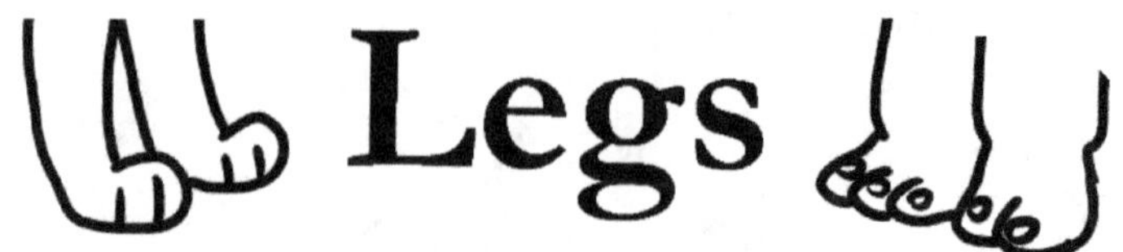

Animal legs can bend forwards...

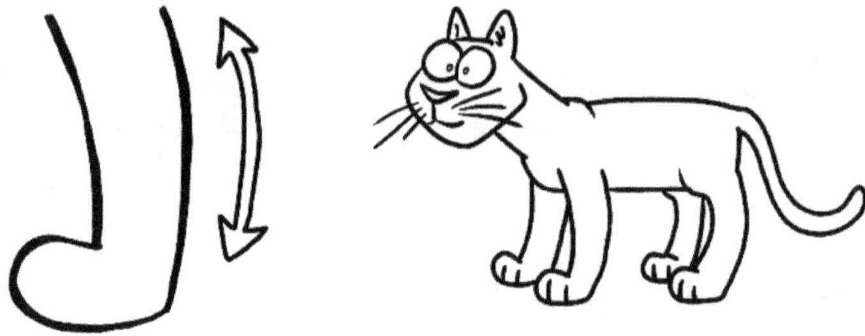

Backwards...

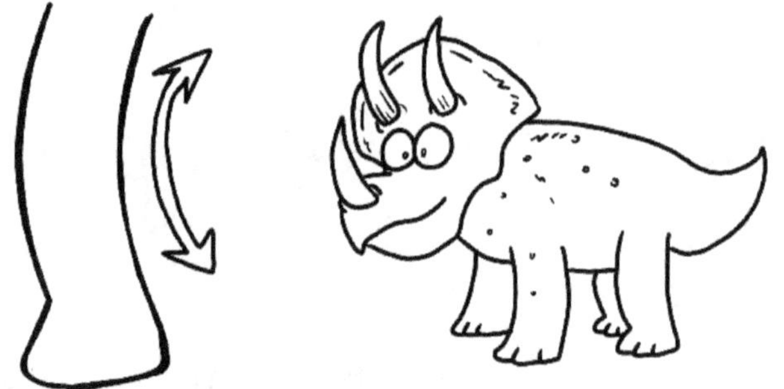

Go straight up and down...

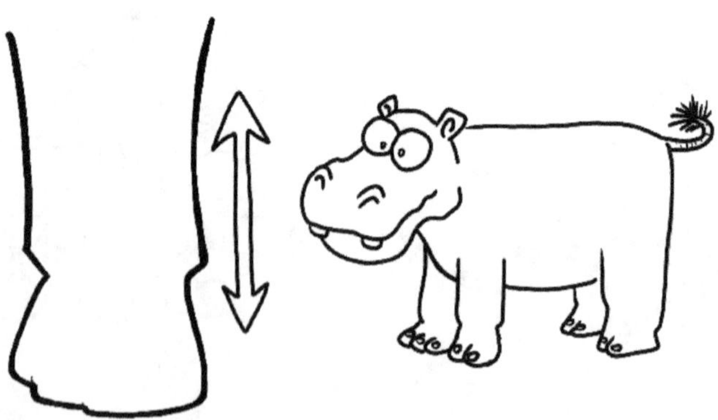

Be bendy…

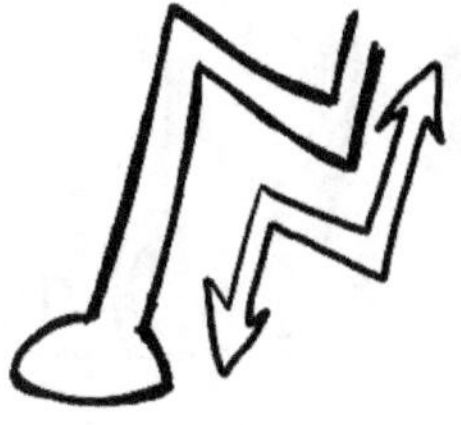

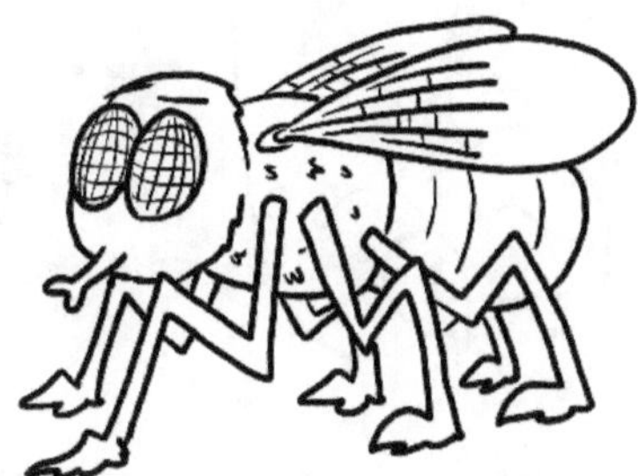

Wavy…

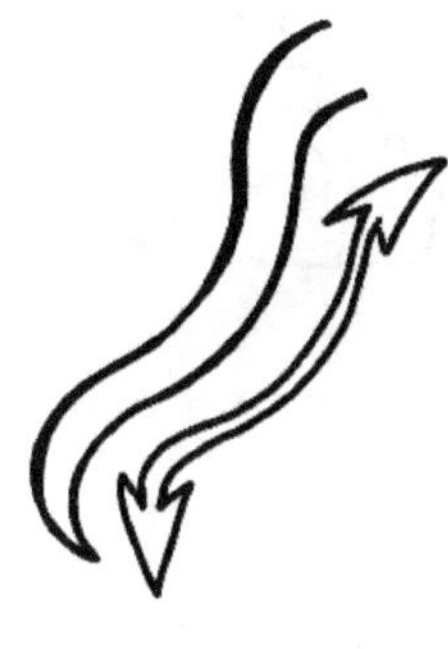

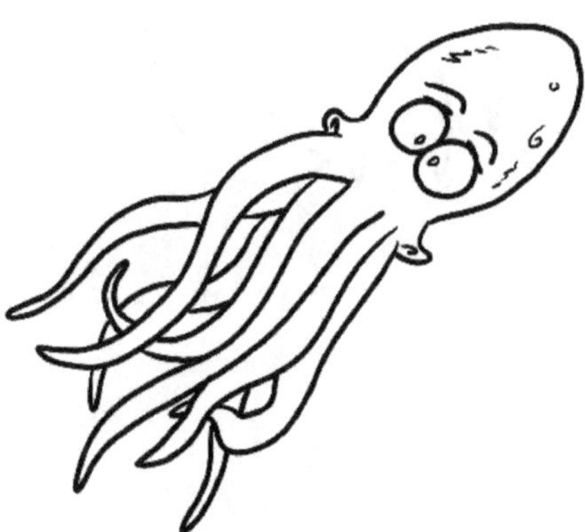

Or bend down.

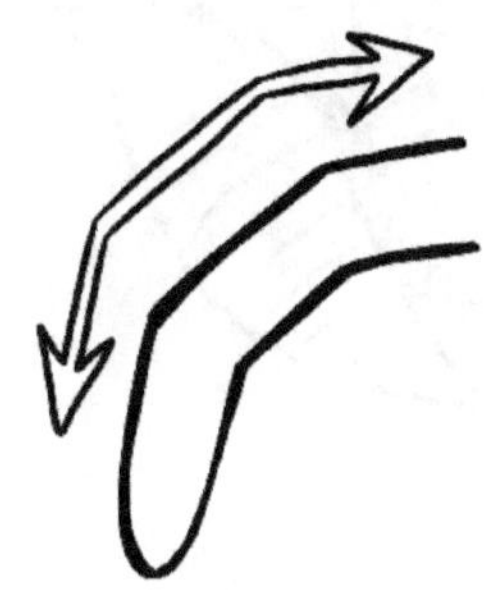

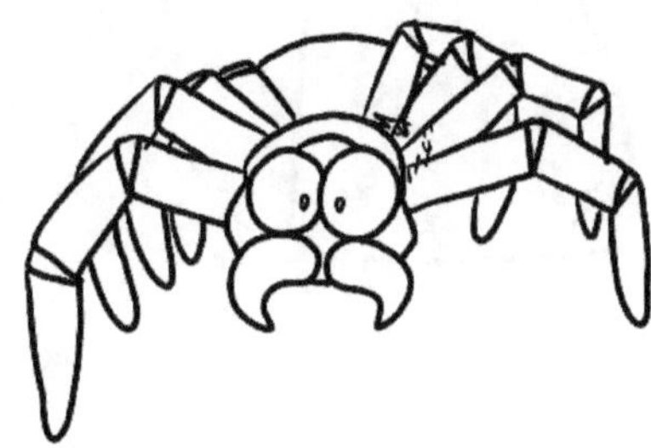

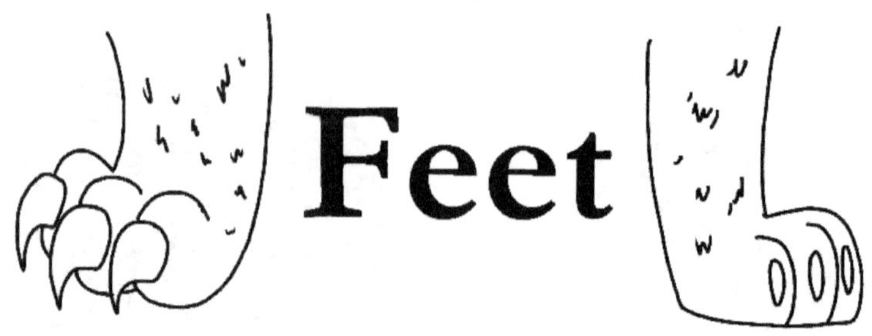

Feet

Legs can have feet with claws or flippers…

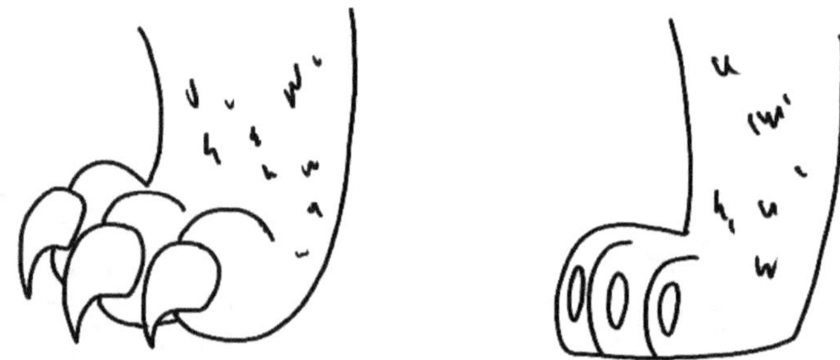

Hooves (one or two toes)…

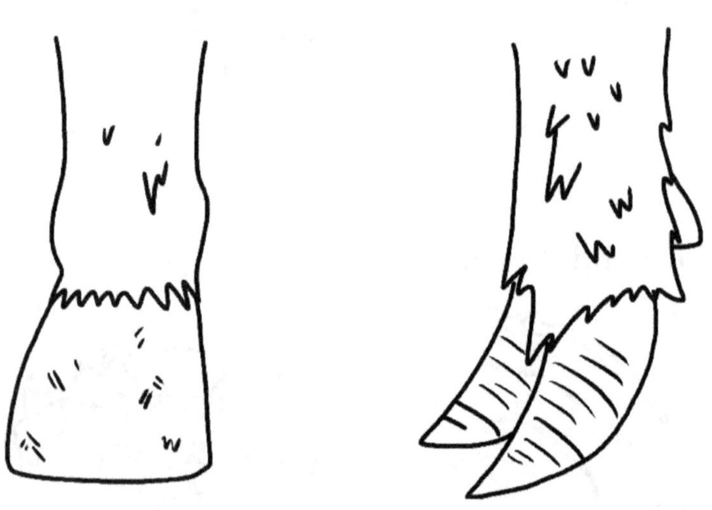

Bug feet like insects and spiders…

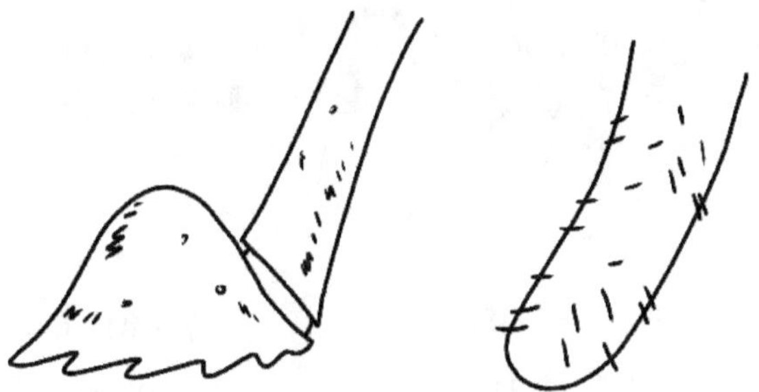

They can almost have people hands or
clawed bird feet…

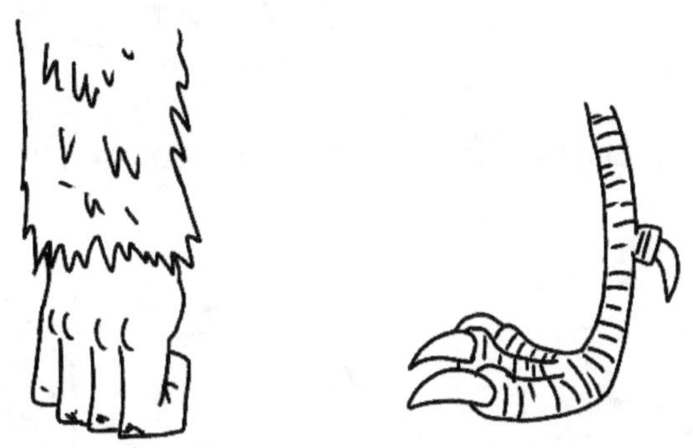

And pincers or tentacles…

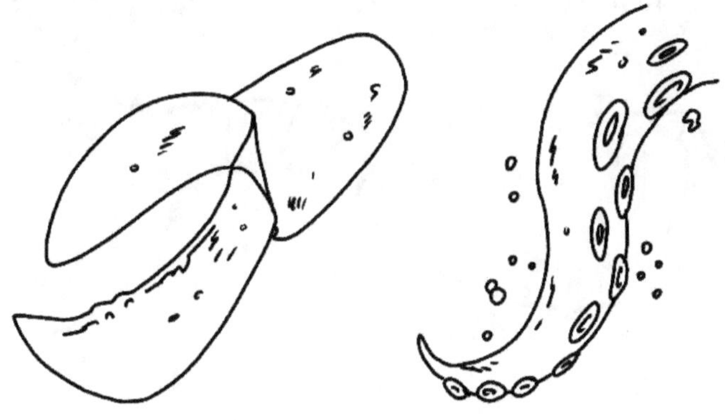

Tails

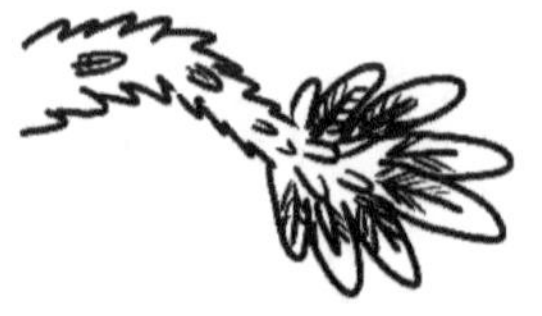

Tails are just sausages, but they can be long or short and sharp-tipped or round-tipped.

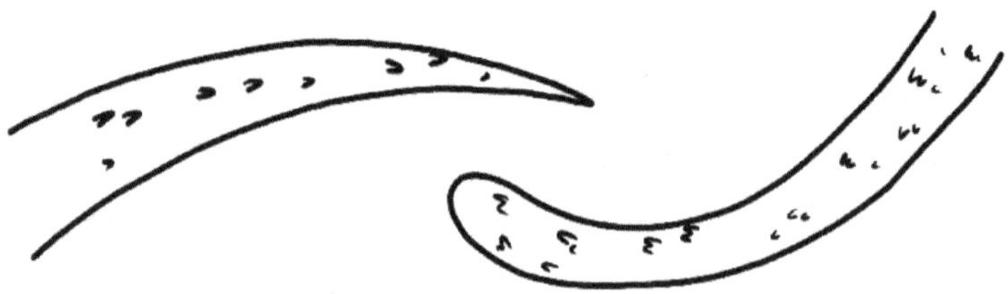

Or they could flare out with fur or feathers.

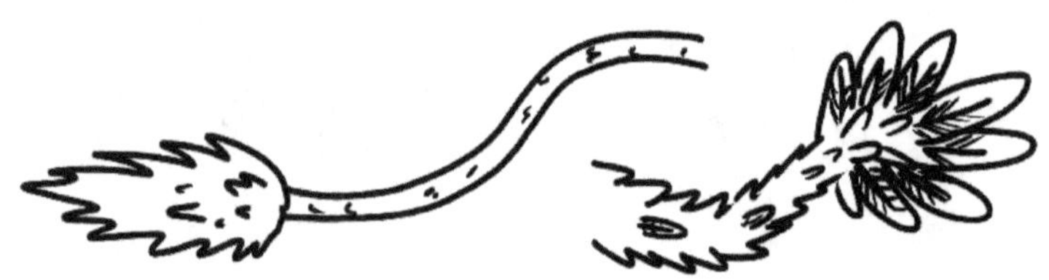

They could have hardly any fur like rat tails…

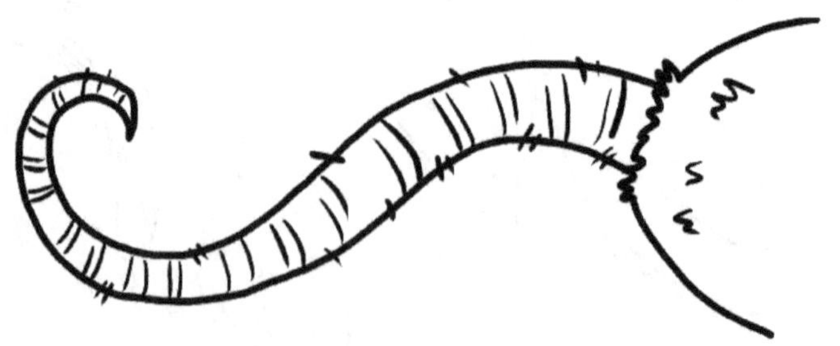

They could end in spikes…

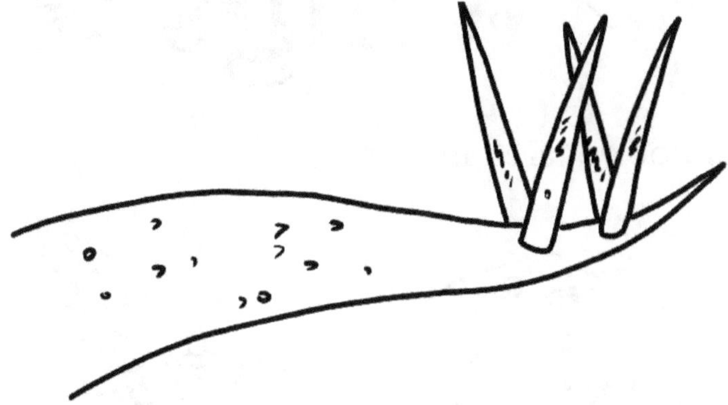

A big ball of bone…

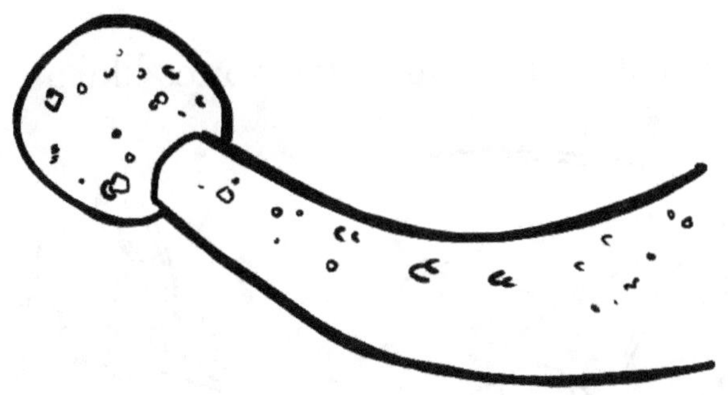

Or even a sting.

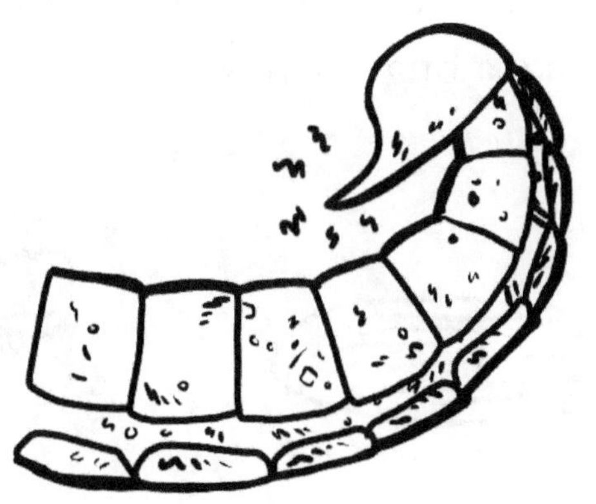

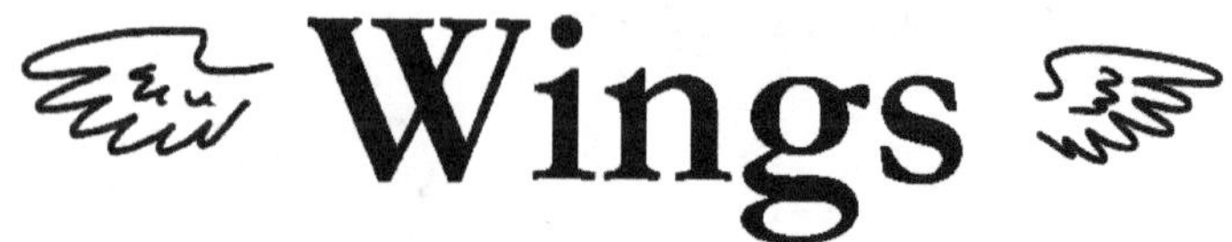

Wings

Can be covered in feathers…

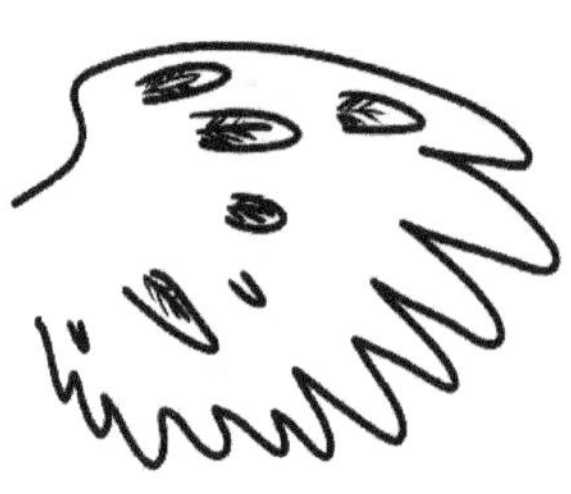

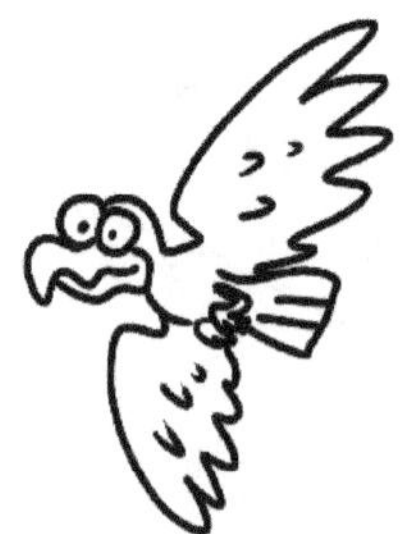

Or skin stretched out over bones like a bat…

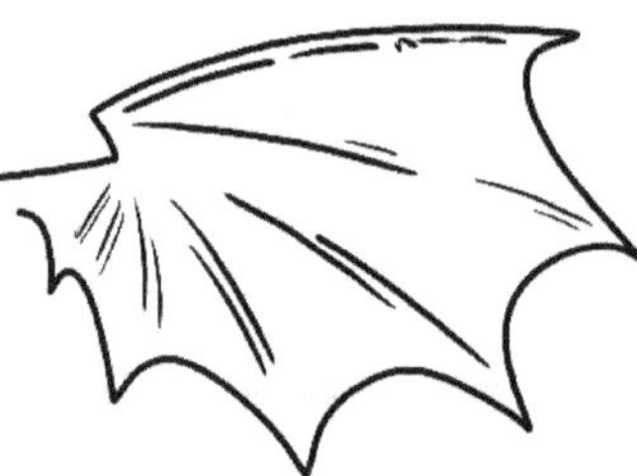

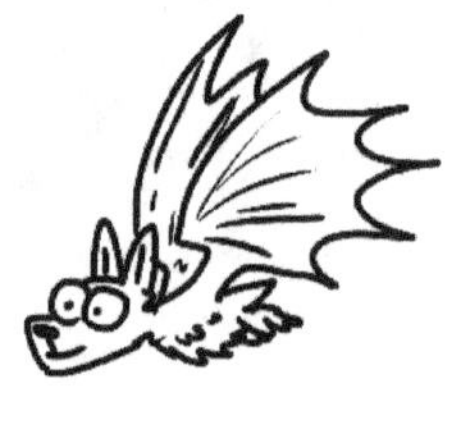

Or they could be see-through with little lines in them like a bug's wings.

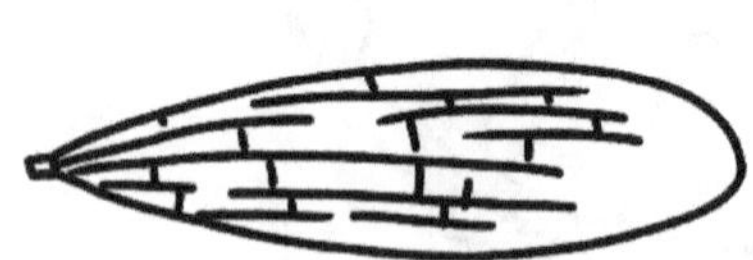

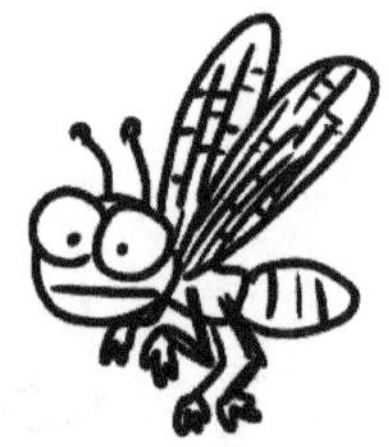

Fins

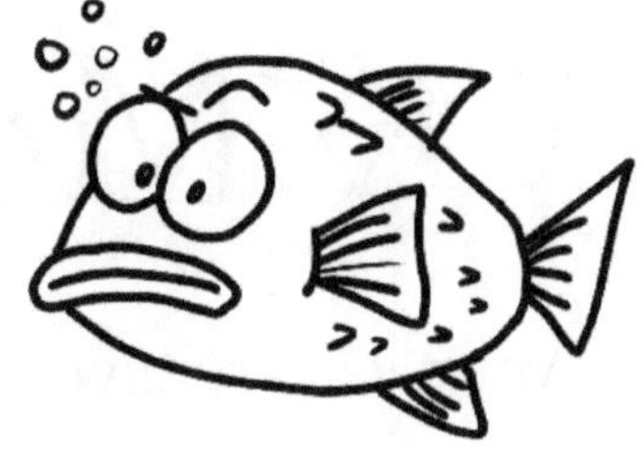

Fins are for swimming. They can have little rays sticking out of them…

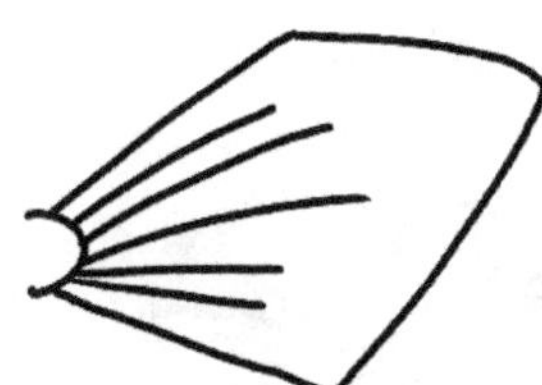

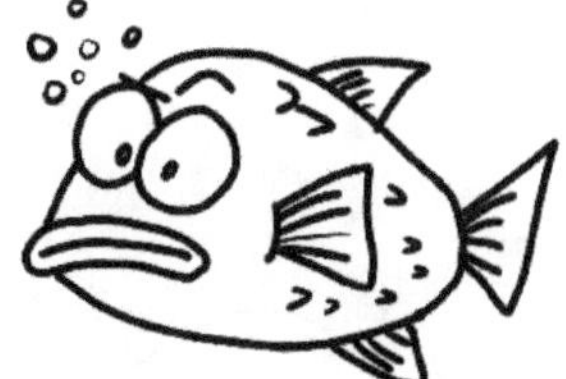

Or they could be covered in the same stuff the rest of the body is covered in…

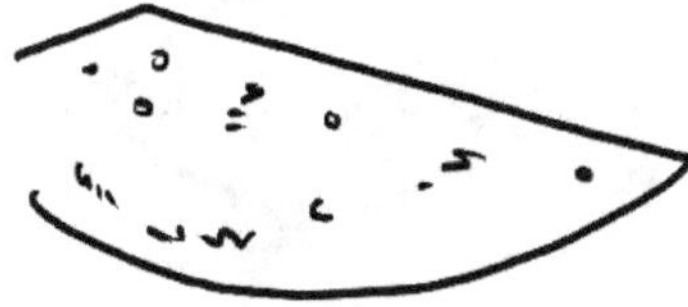

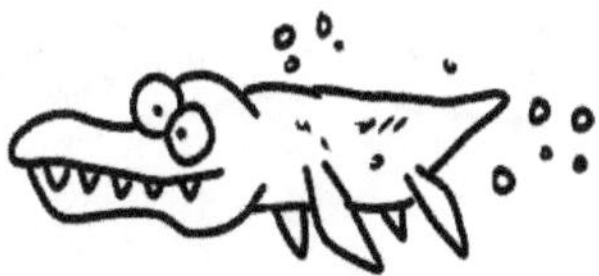

I ran out of fins to add to this page so now there's this blank space that has no purpose.

How are you? Feeling good? Great let's get to the next page.

Mouths

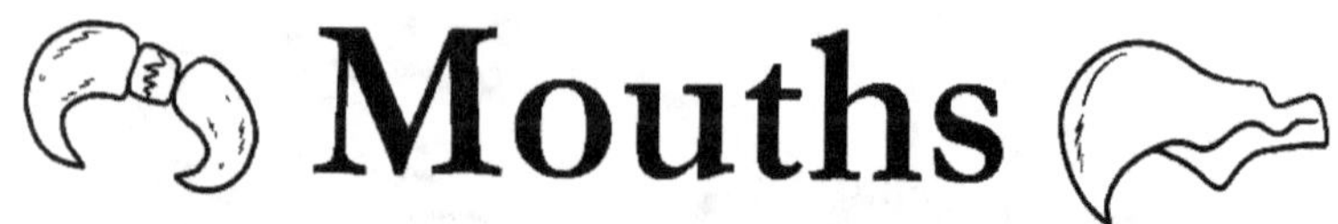

Animals can have toothy mouths…

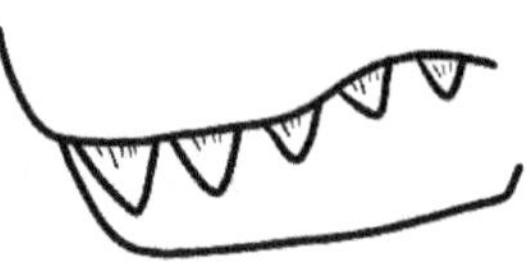
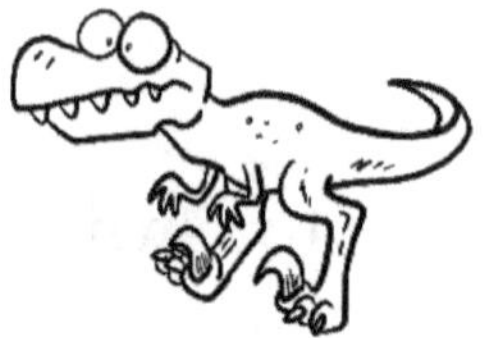

They can have beaks like birds…

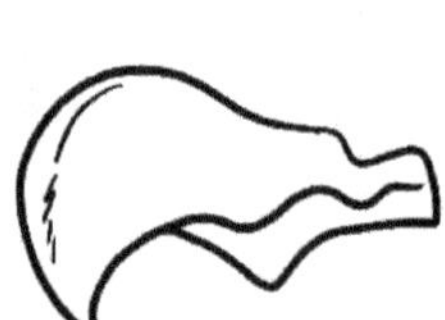
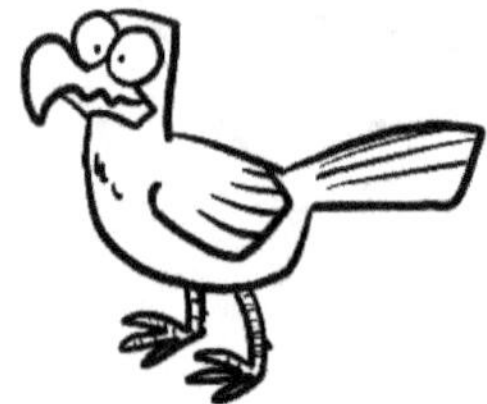

Or toothless lips like fish…

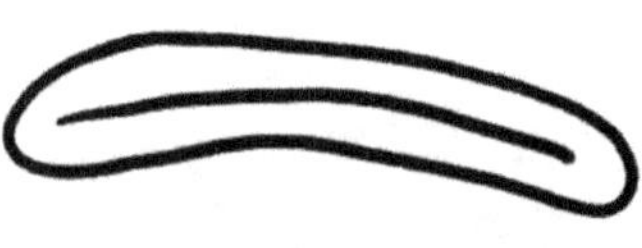
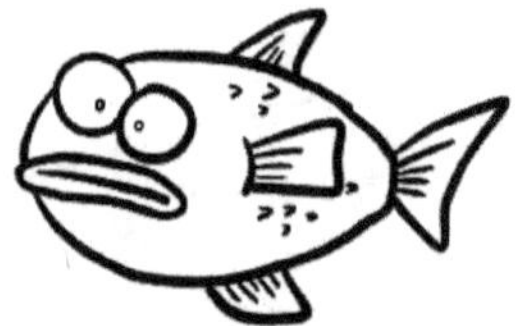

Or fangs like beetles and other bugs.

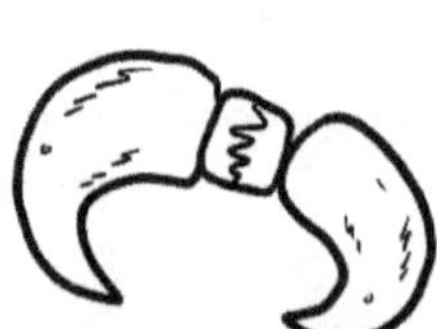
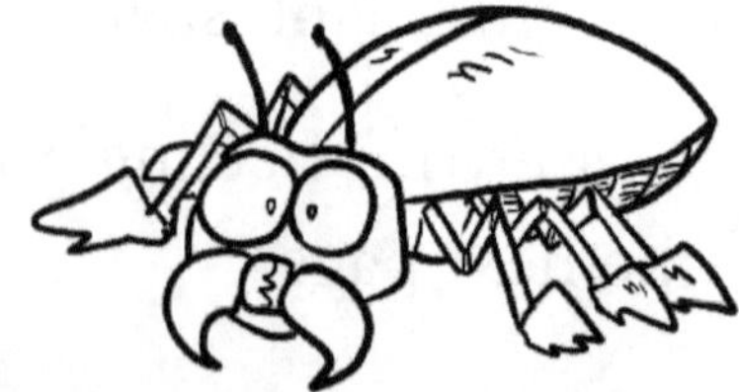

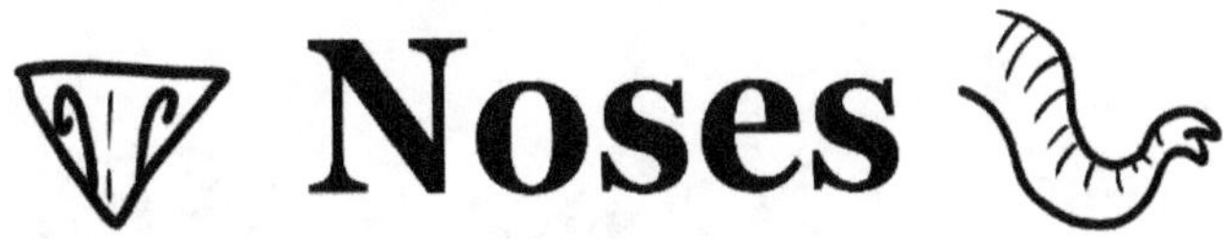 Noses

Noses can be upside down triangles like dogs or cats…

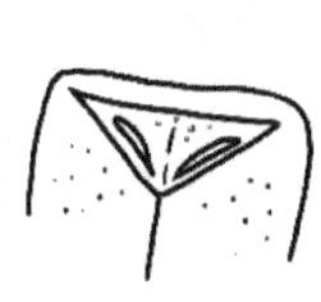

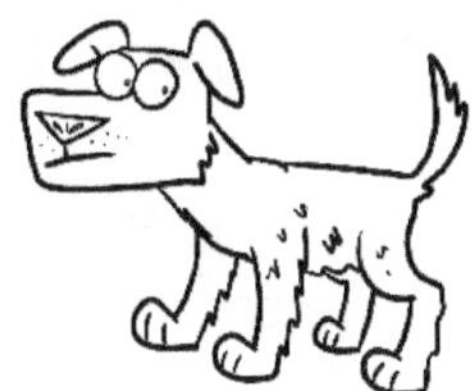

They can be snouts like pigs…

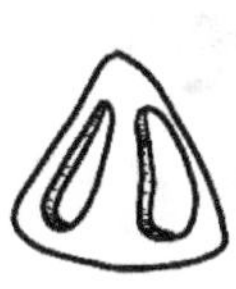

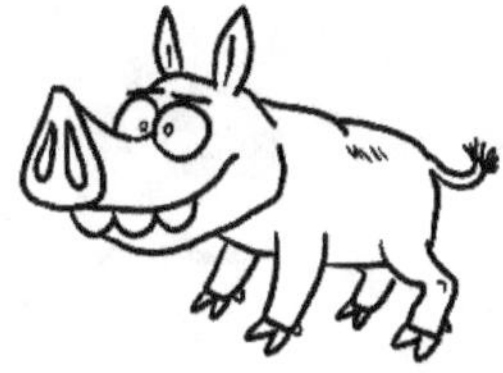

Trunks like elephants…

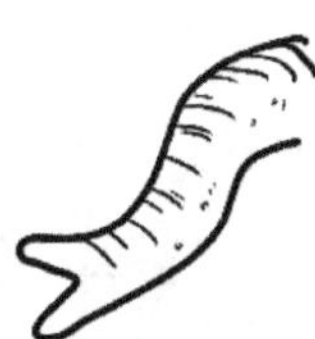

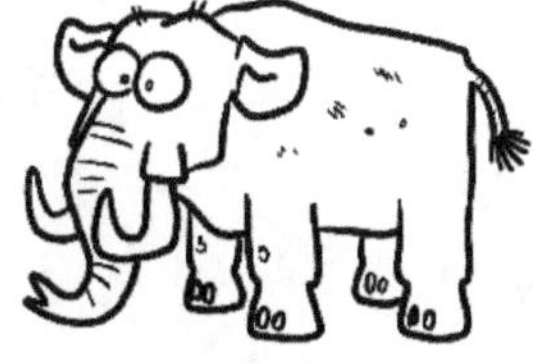

They can just be two slits like lizards or monkeys.

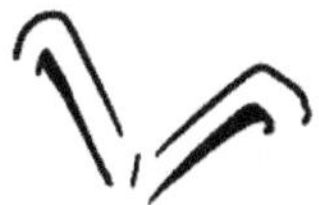

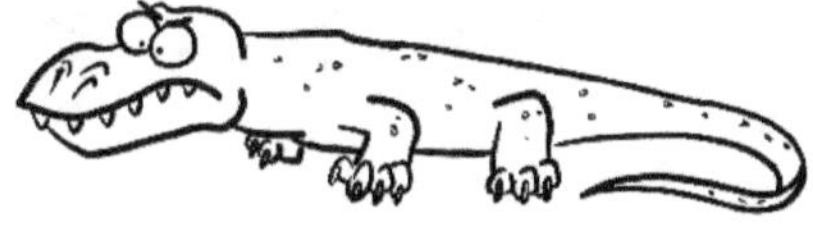

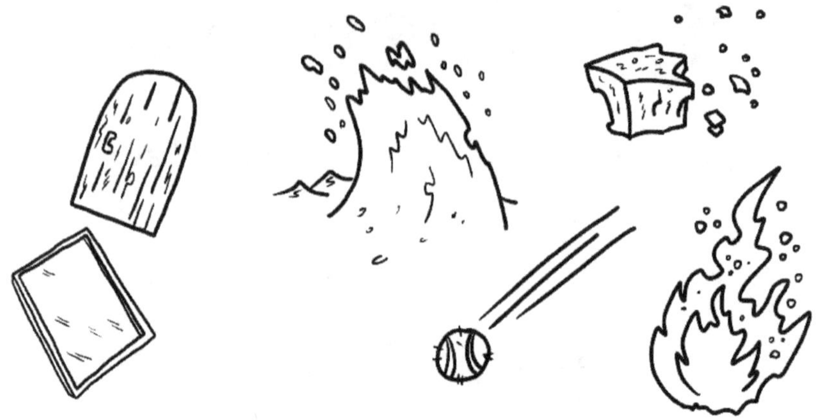

Random Stuff

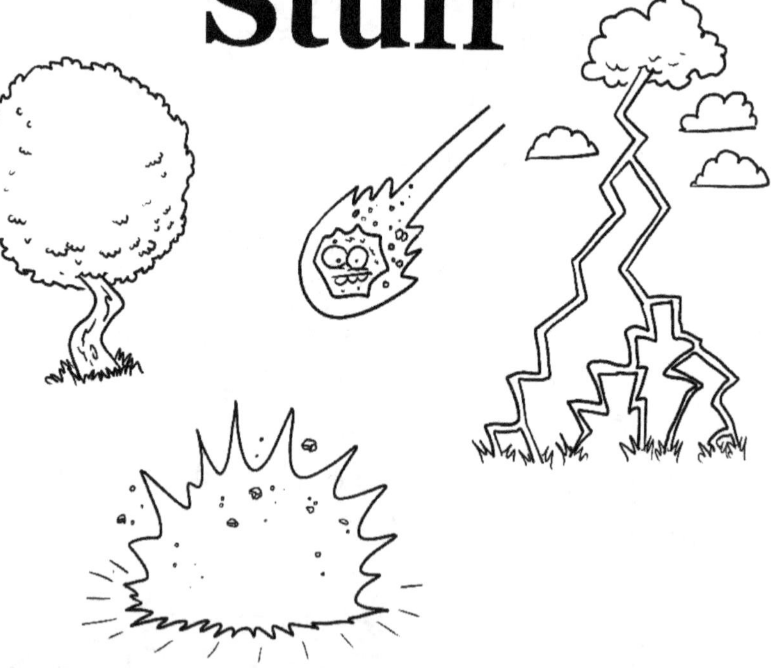

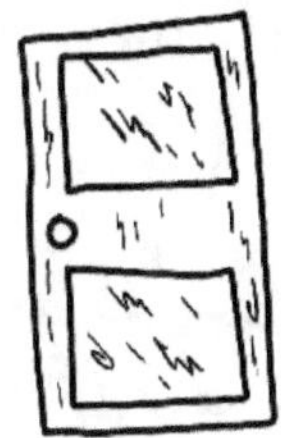 # Building Stuff 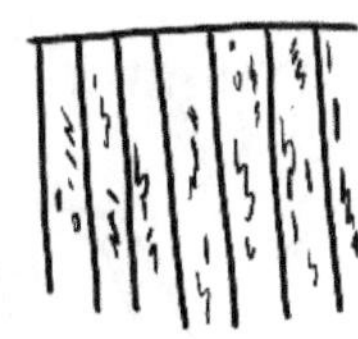

Buildings usually start with a square or rectangle as their shape…

And then I just add stuff…

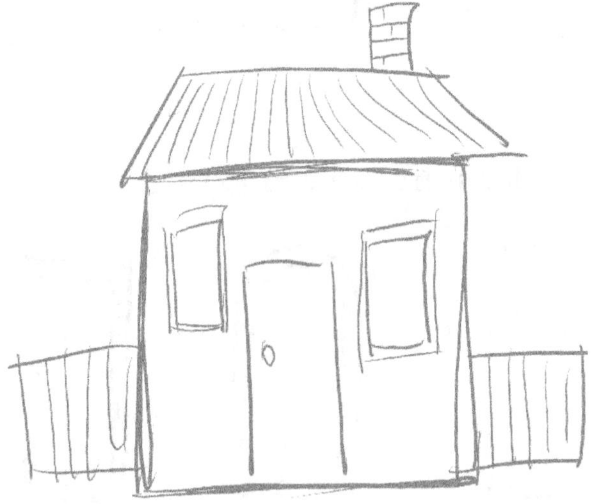

You could start with bigger stuff like a corrugated roof or a tiled roof…

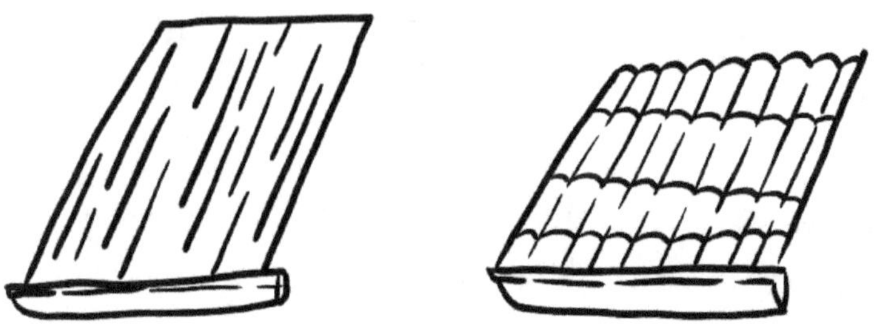

Then you might want to add a door…

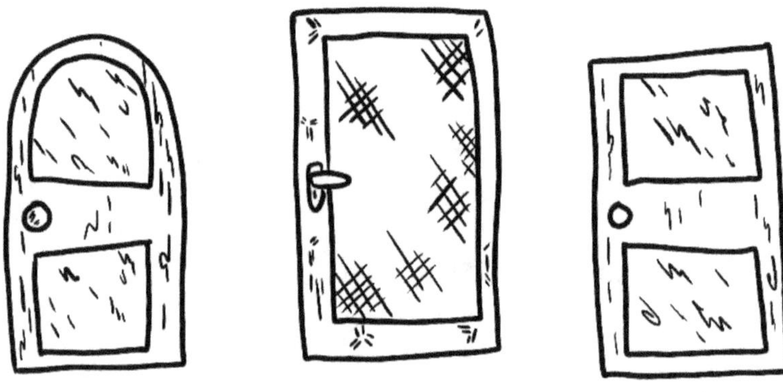

Or smaller stuff like windows…

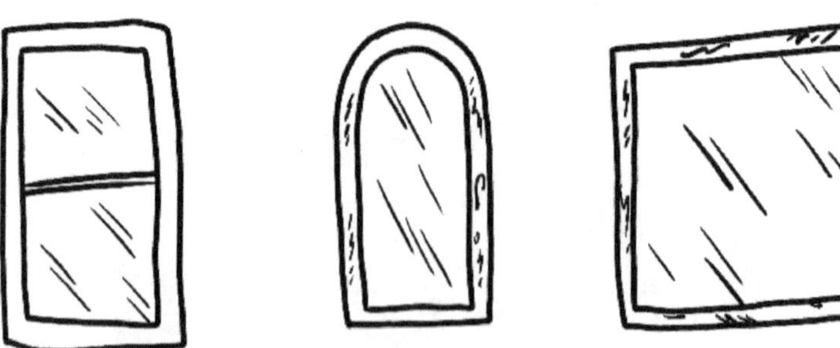

Chimneys and stuff that sticks out of the roof like a pipe or sunlight…

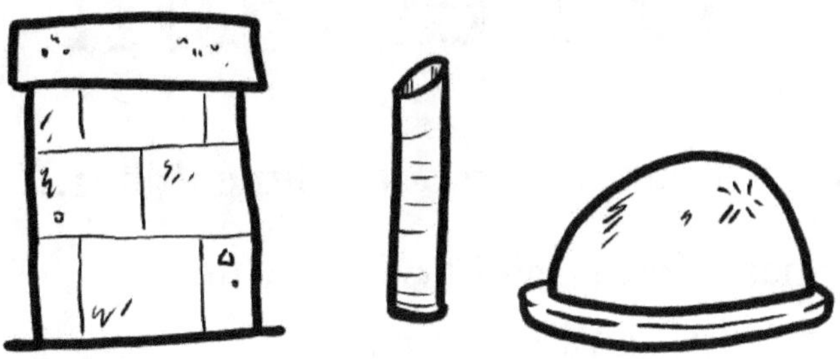

Letterboxes…

Fences…

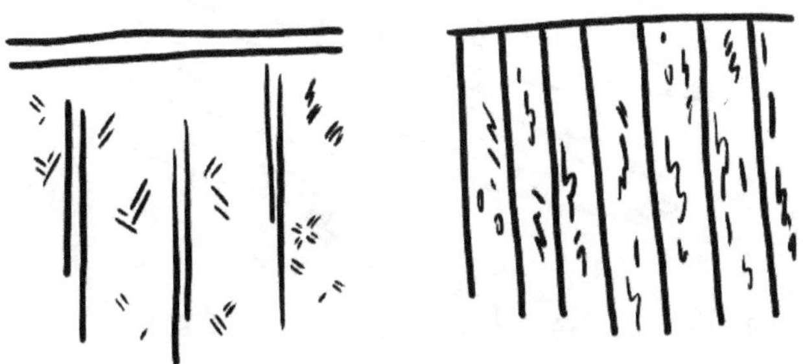

Just remember to include texture when you draw them. Buildings need lots of texture.

Challenge:

Create a road of ten different buildings.

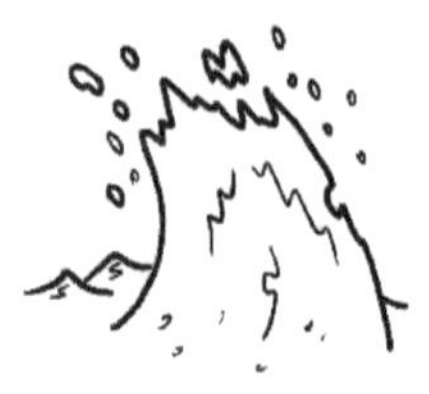# Other Stuff 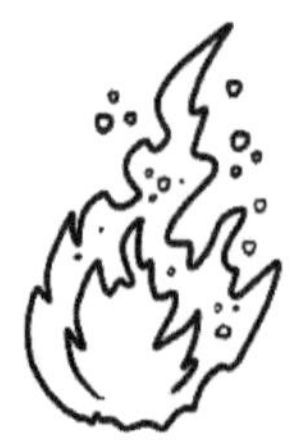

Here's a bunch of random little things…

Air has a few straight or curvy lines can show where the wind is blowing.

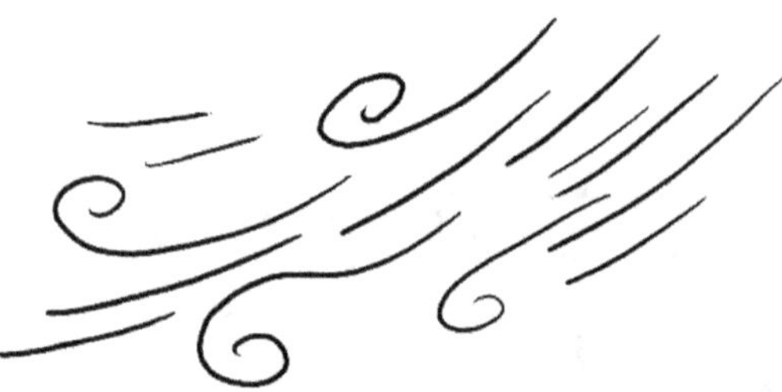

When the wind is strong there are less curly lines and more straight lines…

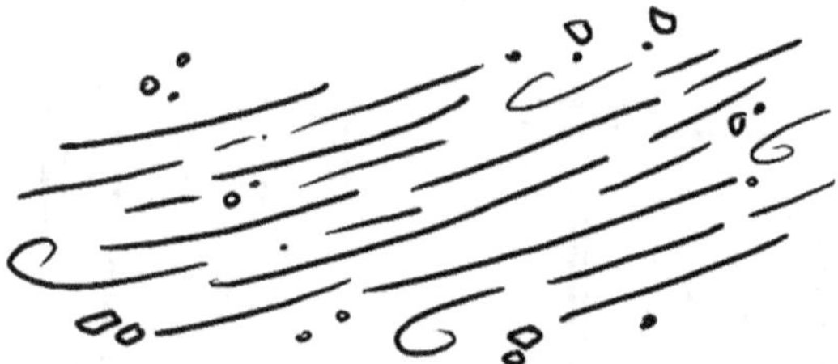

Plants have lots of curves and texture.

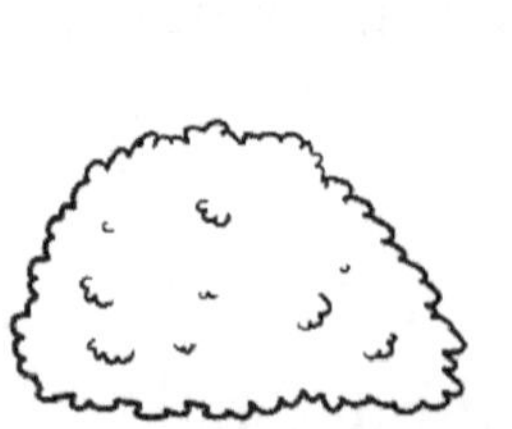 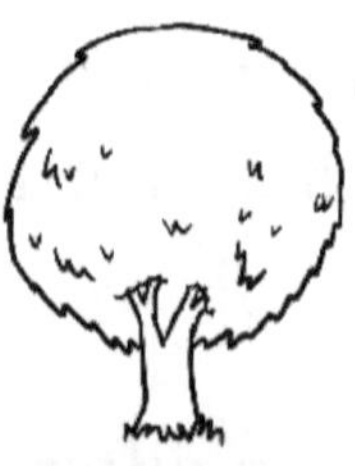 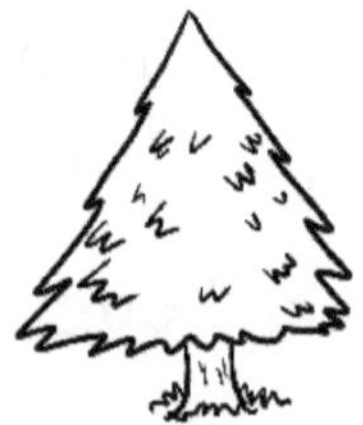

Earth has lots of lines that are almost straight and lots of rock texture.

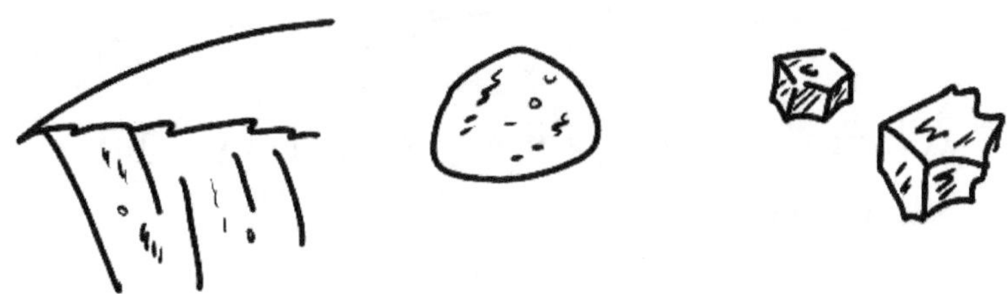

Electricity has lots of jagged sharp pointy sausages. No curves.

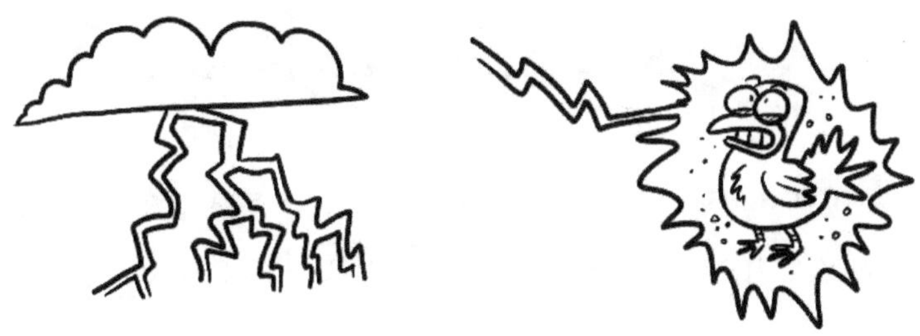

Fire can have straight lines or curvy lines but they have to be ALL curvy or ALL straight.

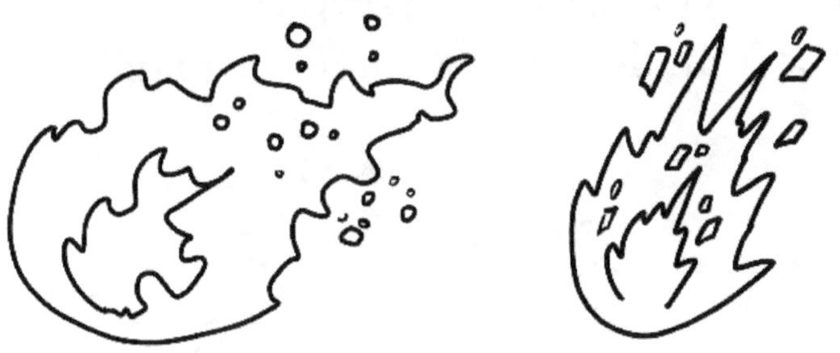

Water is always curvy and every so often
with little bubbles in it.

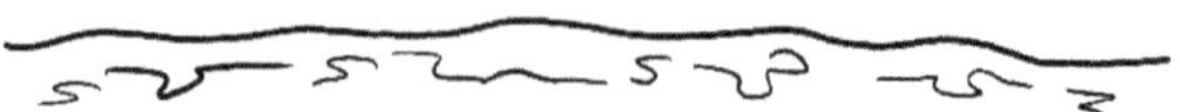

When water gets a little wild, you see little
waves forming…

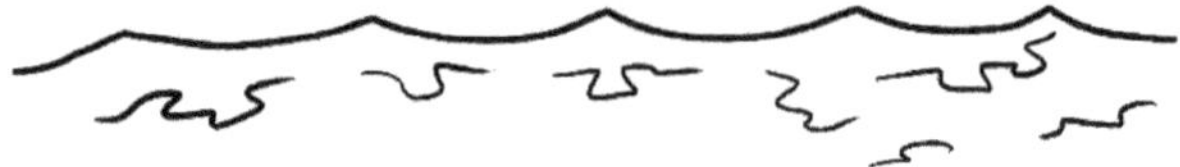

Then there's a bit of splashing and spray.

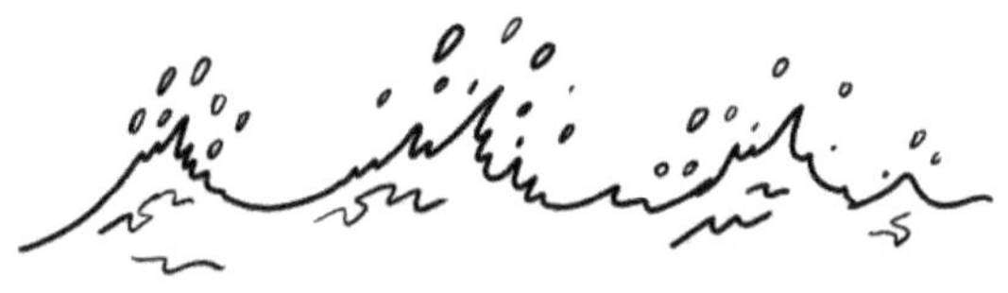

When something bursts out of water, water
and drops all spray out from the same spot.

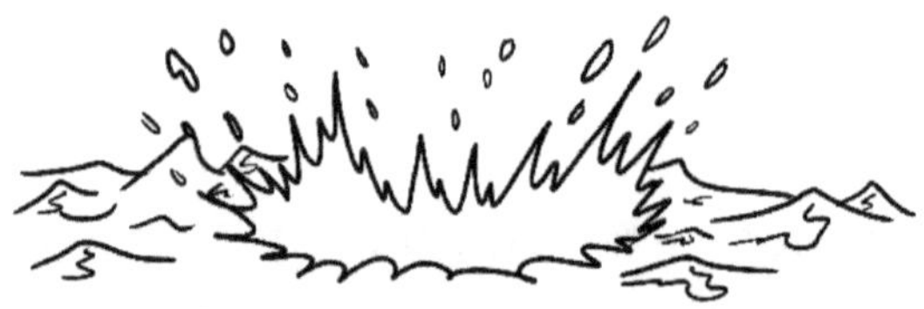

If something explodes, everything shoots
out from the same point in the middle.

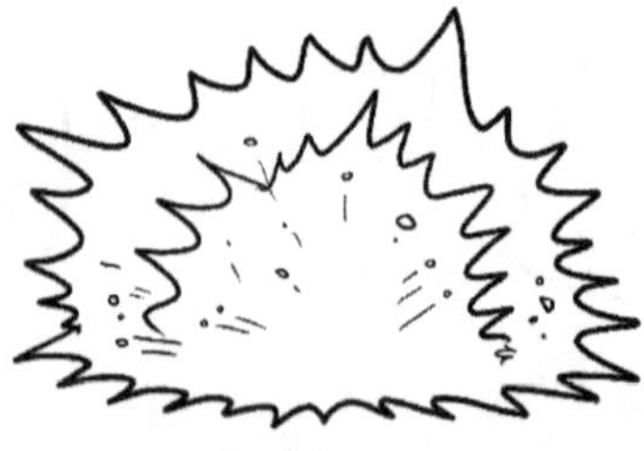

Some lines show something is moving a little.

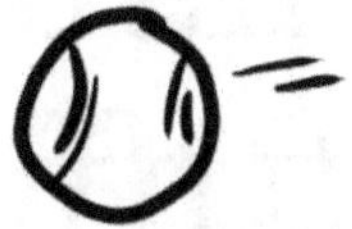

And the more something moves, the more
lines you add…

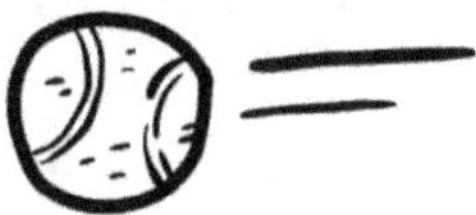

This ball is moving really quickly.

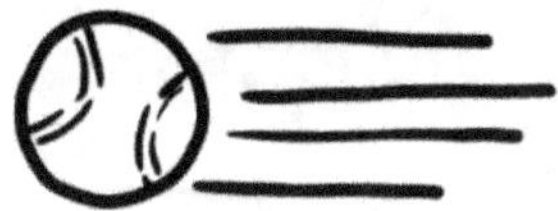

Now this ball is moving so fast, the air is
curling off the front of it…

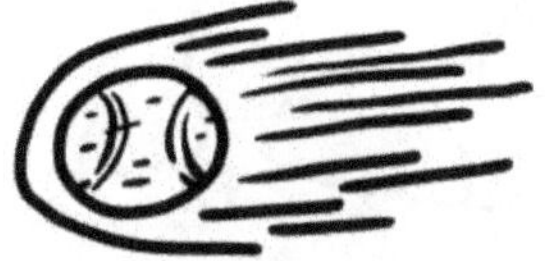

The meteor is moving so fast it is even lit
up with fire and bits are falling off it.

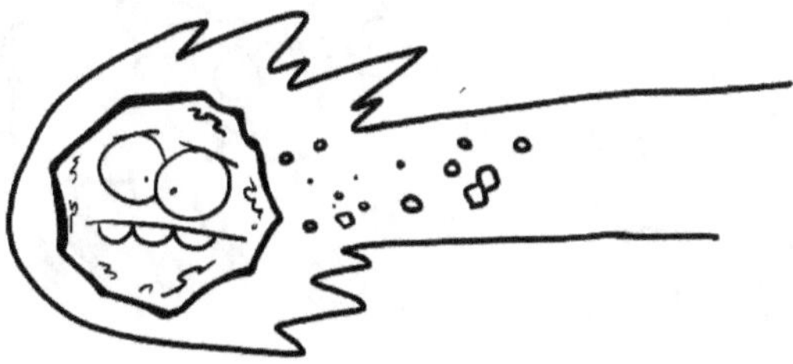

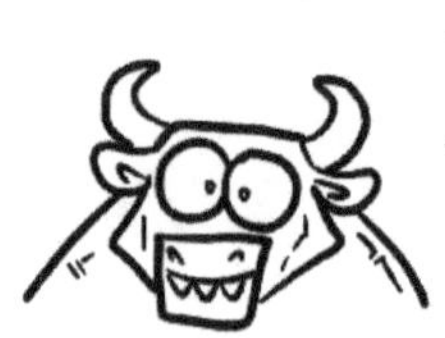 # Monster Stuff 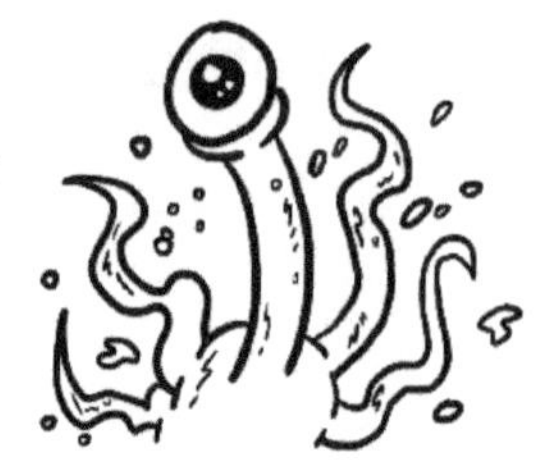

Monsters are a mixture of things that don't normally go together.

Look at this monster- the Minotaur.

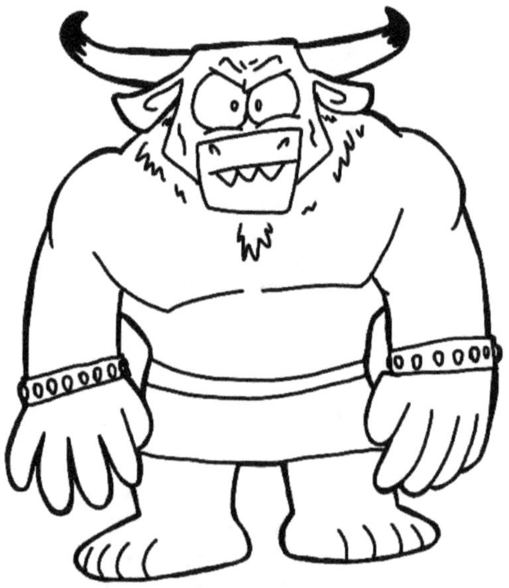

It's just a bull and person mixed together…

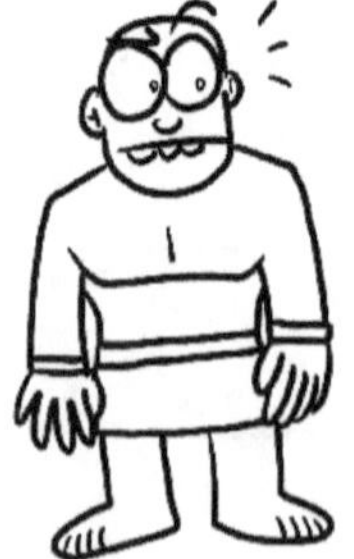 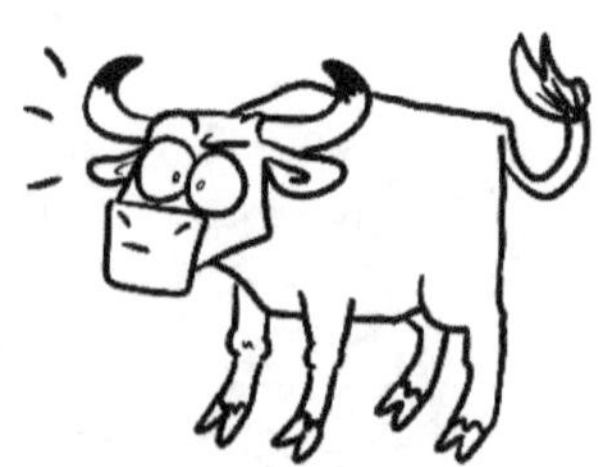

If you want to make a new monster just take things that don't normally go together and stick them together. Like these monsters…

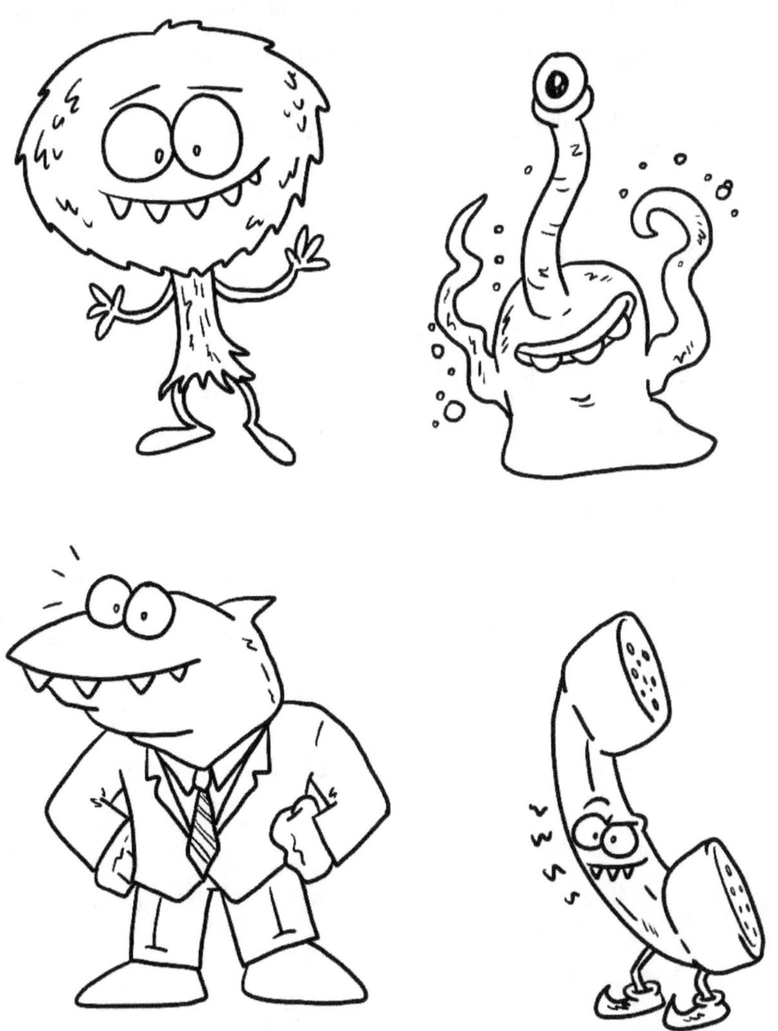

Challenge:

Create ten new monsters with different bits. They don't have to make sense at all.

Well, that's it.

There's not much more to tell you about drawing except for a few thoughts…

Keep drawing over and over.

Don't listen to people that tell you that you're no good at drawing.

If you draw something that you don't think is very good just draw another picture until you create something you like.

Then take a break.

If there's any skill or idea I haven't covered that you want to know about just send me an email:

thatdavidconley@gmail.com

Also by David Conley

That Book About Norse Mythology: Part 1

That Book About Norse Mythology: Part 2

That Book About Greek Mythology: Part 1

That Book About Greek Mythology: Part 2

That Book About Egyptian Mythology

That Book About Space Stuff

That Activity Book About Norse Mythology

That Activity Book About Greek Mythology

About the Author

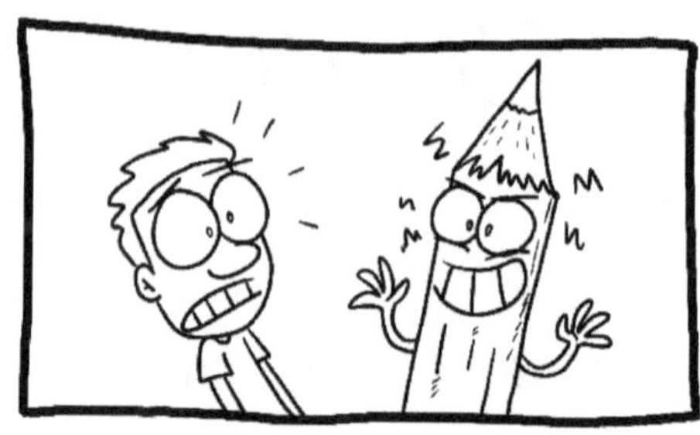

From a young age, David has drawn pictures and written stories to entertain friends and family.

He also drew stories and wrote pictures until he was informed this was physically impossible.

David didn't give up, though, and he tried to change the laws of physics. Unfortunately, David accidentally changed the laws a little too much and turned himself into a bright blue potato.

David still loves to draw and write.

Find him on Instagram:

@thatdavidconley

Or just shoot him an email:

thatdavidconley@gmail.com